ROYAL GEOGRAPHICAL SOCIETY
# ILLUSTRATED

Created by Co & Bear Productions (U.K.) Ltd.
Copyright © 1997 Co & Bear Productions Ltd.
Photographs copyright © Royal Geographical Society
© Royal Geographical Society (Development Ltd.)
All rights reserved.

First published in the U.K. in 1997 by Scriptum Editions,
a trading division of Co & Bear Productions Ltd.
Richmond House, St. Anne's Place,
St. Peter Port, Guernsey, GY1 3YS, U.K.

Published and distributed in the U.S. in 1998 by
Stewart, Tabori & Chang,
a division of U.S. Media Holdings, Inc.
115 West 18th Street, New York, NY 10011

Distributed in Canada by General Publishing Company Ltd.
30 Lesmill Road, Don Mills, Ontario, Canada M3B 2T6

U.K. Publisher *Beatrice Vincenzini*
Creative Director *Charles Orchard*
Project Manager *David Shannon*
Designers *Paul Ashby, Emma Skidmore*
Jacket Designer for U.S. Edition *Lisa Vaughn*
Consulting Editor *Dr. John Hemming*
Editors *Diana Craig, Jenny Vaughan, Alexandra Black, Laura Ivill*
Picture Researchers *Cee Weston-Baker, Rupert Tenison*
Publishing Assistant *Emma Head*

The publishers, editors, and the Royal Geographical Society
are not responsible for the opinions or statements of
contributors to the *Royal Geographical Society Illustrated*.

ISBN: 1-55670-817-3
Library of Congress Catalog Card Number: 97–62391

Printed in Italy
10  9  8  7  6  5  4  3  2  1

# ROYAL GEOGRAPHICAL SOCIETY
# ILLUSTRATED

STEWART, TABORI & CHANG
NEW YORK

# contents

The archaeologist Sir Alfred Percival Maudslay (*opposite*), who made several expeditions to explore the ancient cultures of Central America, is seen here, in about 1889, at work in Mayan ruins in Yucatan, Mexico. Photograph by H. N. Sweet.

# foreword

## Lord Jellicoe

IT IS A GREAT HONOUR TO BE ABLE to contribute my small offering – the foreword – to this book which illustrates the long history of worldwide exploration carried out since 1830 under the aegis of the Royal Geographical Society.

The Society has a splendid inheritance – its fine buildings, its famous library, its archives and its 900,000 maps. Perhaps less well known is its collection of pictures and its half a million photographs of explorers and exploration – the greatest collection of its kind in the world. It is clearly our duty not only to preserve these unique collections but also to make them better known and more accessible.

In this book some of our greatest explorers and mountaineers, in introducing the photographs in our collection, recount their impressions and experiences in their own inimitable way. For example, Edmund Hillary tells us what India and Nepal, their people and their mountains, mean to him. From Ranulph Fiennes we learn the power of the Norwegian term *polarhulle* – 'a yearning forever to return to the far, dark, cold places'. With Wilfred Thesiger we cross for the first time the Empty Quarter which for him was, with typical understatement, 'a personal experience and the reward had been a drink of clear, tasteless water. I was content with that.' And from John Hemming, our eminent Director for twenty-one years, we have his telling comment on the great Maraca Rainforest Project in Amazonia: 'It is such work which makes the present day the golden age of discovery, the time when human beings are learning more than ever before about the natural wonders of the planet.'

Few of the photographs shown have ever before seen the light of day in book form. The choice has necessarily been selective. I believe, however, that they represent the cream of a vast photographic collection which evokes not only the spirit of exploration, with all its challenges and hazards, but also the special quality of the desert, mountain and polar landscape seen in some instances for the first time by human eye and by the eye of a camera. Moreover, as Michael Freeman, in his fascinating chapter on the evolution of photography makes clear, these pictures record not only the history of exploration and some of its more dramatic moments but also the history of photography itself. As Freeman rightly states, when photography and camera were in their infancy 'using a camera on location called for heroic efforts on the part of the photographer'.

I have to confess to some special favourites among the photographs in this book. For example, I would take to my desert island that picture so redolent of Imperial calm and grandeur by V. C. Scott O'Connor (page 52), Hillary's famous Mount Everest shot of Tenzing (page 74), Frank Hurley's photograph (page 169) of Shackleton's return from his epic journey to South Georgia, Chris Bradley's evocation of Yemeni architecture (page 229) and the lovely Ethiopian girl by L. Naretti and G. P. Devey (page 114). However I leave it to the reader to make his or her own choice.

RGS President 1993-1997

Jellicoe

# introduction

## Dr. John Hemming

WHEN THE ROYAL GEOGRAPHICAL SOCIETY was founded under Royal Charter in 1830, it had a clear mission: to promote 'that most important and entertaining branch of knowledge – geography'. This is an educational role which the Society continues to fulfil in many ways – through lectures and conferences, through the publication of learned journals and books, in contacts with teachers and government, and by amassing and maintaining world-famous collections of maps, books, archives and pictures. In 1995, its academic standing was further confirmed by the merger with The Institute of British Geographers.

Despite the importance of this work, it is not for its educational contribution that the Society is renowned, but for its central role in the exploration of the world. Born out of an explorers' dining club, the RGS started to support expeditions immediately after its foundation, to receive reports from returning explorers, and to honour the lucky ones with medals. As a race, the British excel as explorers and the Royal Geographical Society has been involved in discoveries by Europeans in every far-flung corner of our planet and the filling-in of many of the blanks on its map. All of these expeditions have involved challenge and personal danger. Some ended in triumph, some in disaster, but many have earned a place in the history books and all have contributed to our knowledge and understanding of the planet on which we live.

During its almost-170-year history different regions have claimed the focus of the Society's attention. For many decades, one of the most elusive goals for explorers was to find the Northwest Passage through the uncharted archipelago of islands north of Canada. In 1845 the Society's Vice President Sir John Franklin took up the challenge. With 138 men and two steam-sailing ships specially designed for polar service, he set off to try to find the hoped-for route. He never returned. After eight years of silence, he and his men were presumed dead. Successive attempts to find them, by sea and overland across the Canadian tundra, revealed tragic graves and other relics.

Both failure and success attended expeditions at the opposite side of the globe, where explorers were penetrating the deserts of the Australian outback. Various teams sought to cross the continent, partly to see whether it contained a central lake. The Royal Geographical Society did not organise or finance these ventures, but it was generous in honouring Australian explorers. Burke and Wills, the first to cross Australia from south to north, died in the attempt. But others – among them Eyre, Leichhardt, Sturt, Stuart, the Gregory brothers, Giles and Gibson – received gold medals. The Society's resident artist Thomas Baines was with the Gregorys in Northern Australia, and his dramatic paintings of their discoveries are treasures of the picture collection.

Also in the southern hemisphere at that time, Captain Robert Fitzroy charted the coasts of southern South America in HMS *Beagle,* accompanied by his friend Charles Darwin. We all know how momentous that voyage was in inspiring the seminal theory of evolution by natural selection. In 1849 three young Englishmen - Alfred Wallace, Henry Bates and Richard Spruce – arrived in the Amazon and embarked on years of stupendous collecting of its flora and fauna. Bates returned to London to become the Society's first paid Secretary, and Wallace went to Southeast Asia (assisted by the RGS) to evolve the same theory as Darwin.

In the middle decades of the nineteenth century, attention turned to central Africa. In the 1850s, the satanic-looking Richard Burton moved from fascination with Islam and the sexual mysteries of southern Asia to a personal quest for the source of the Nile. The RGS was closely involved in all this. It backed Burton and his bluff companion John Speke, and then sponsored Speke and Grant when they succeeded in finding the Nile's outflow from the lake which they named after Queen Victoria. Another explorer, the genial big-game hunter Samuel Baker, advanced up the Nile from the Sudan. He was accompanied by his beautiful young wife Florence, whom he had acquired in the Balkans. Florence delighted the Africans by washing her long blonde hair, and her charm and cool judgment repeatedly saved the couple from tight corners – she would be top of my personal team of 'fantasy expeditioners'. The RGS has a delightful collection of Baker's naïve but vigorous watercolours.

Meanwhile, farther south, Dr. David Livingstone was crossing the Kalahari desert and making an amazing traverse of the Dark Continent from Angola to the mouth of the Zambezi. Livingstone was a humanitarian who fought the slave trade and he was an incomparable explorer – but as a missionary his score of converts was almost nil. The RGS helped to build a boat for Dr. Livingstone to return to the Zambezi. The artist Thomas

Baines made vivid paintings of that voyage and the first European views of Victoria Falls, many of which adorn the walls of the Society's headquarters. Alongside these is a case in which are sometimes displayed the hats worn by Livingstone and Stanley at their famous meeting at Ujiji in 1871, when the ill and ageing Livingstone was also searching for a source of the Nile. When the great man died two years later, his faithful retainers buried Livingstone's entrails under a tree and carried his body across Africa to the Indian Ocean, for shipment to England where it lay in state in the Society's building. That actual tree is now also in the Society's House.

Throughout the later nineteenth and early twentieth centuries, the farthest points of our planet, the North and South Poles, attracted explorers. The polar prizes eluded the British, however. The American Commander Robert Peary (or possibly his compatriot Dr. Frederick Cook) was the first to the North Pole, in 1909; two years later, the Norwegian Roald Amundsen reached the South Pole just before Scott. But the British, under the Society's later president Vivian Fuchs, organised the first crossing of Antarctica in 1955-58; and Ranulph Fiennes's Transglobe Expedition in the 1980s was the first to traverse both poles.

Recent decades have witnessed the world's greatest flowering of exploration. We live in the golden age of discovery, but the finest modern investigations are scientific. These identify thousands of species of animal and insect new to science, understand the functioning of the great ecosystems - rainforests, deserts, mountain regions, ice-sheets, savannas, wetlands and oceans - and survey the remotest mountain peaks, white-water rivers, forests, caves, or sea beds. The Royal Geographical Society has played a role in this scientific outburst, by assisting hundreds of small research expeditions and by organising its own major projects. There have been a dozen RGS-sponsored projects since I became its Director in 1975, and all have brought fine collections into the picture library. Notable among these were the Mulu (Sarawak) Expedition of 1977-78, the International Karakoram Expedition of 1980, Nigel Winser's Oman Wahiba Project, and my own Maraca Rainforest Project of 1987-88 which deployed almost 200 scientists and technicians in unexplored forests of Brazilian Amazonia.

Throughout its involvement in worldwide exploration, the Royal Geographical Society has been greatly aided by the medium of photography – which came into being not long after the Society itself. In teaching explorers to use it as a research tool to record their findings, the RGS laid the foundations for its own unique photographic library. Many of the later African explorers who were helped by the RGS gave it their pictures or named mountains and rivers after the Society's Presidents. Particularly fine collections of photographs came from Sir Harry Johnson and Ernest Gedge in East Africa, others from Joseph Thompson in Kenya, Courtney Selous in Tanzania, Boyd Alexander in Nigeria and many more. Across the Red Sea in Arabia, St John Philby, Charles Doughty and, later, Freya Stark and Wilfred Thesiger all fell under the spell of the desert and its proud Arab and Bedu inhabitants, and made a photographic record of much of what they saw. Among the Society's most

prized possessions, however, are the superb photographs of the formation of Saudi Arabia taken by Captain Shakespear, who was killed charging into battle with Ibn Saud's camel warriors.

India was the jewel in Queen Victoria's crown, and consequently the Royal Geographical Society has admirable photography of all South Asia. The Society was particularly concerned with the exploration of the Himalayas and the plateau of Central Asia when this was disputed by Russia and Great Britain in the 'Great Game' of imperial geopolitics. The location of Lhasa was as great a geographical prize as the source of the Nile, and the RGS awarded its 1877 gold medal to Nain Singh, the brave pundit who spent years disguised as a Buddhist pilgrim to survey the interior of Tibet. But the Society's greatest picture collections of Asia came later: from Mrs Isabella Bird Bishop, one of the first lady Fellows of the RGS who made romantic and fearless travels in the Rocky Mountains and then in Japan, China and Persia; from Douglas Carruthers, who surveyed deep into Russian Central Asia and Mongolia; and from the great plant collector Frank Kingdon-Ward whose Himalayan flowers have transformed British gardens. There is also a lovely set of watercolours of Nepal in the 1850s by Oldfield.

The great attraction of the Himalayas was its mountains and, of course, the world's highest, named after the Surveyor-General of India, George Everest. The RGS started sponsoring attempts to climb Mount Everest in 1922 and it has photographs from all the subsequent Everest expeditions and from the mountaineering achievements of Eric Shipton and Bill Tilman. These include Shipton's shot of the footprints of the Yeti or

Abominable Snowman, which was probably a hoax. John Hunt's 1953 Everest expedition was planned in a room in the Society's House, and Alfred Gregory's thrilling photographic record of it is in the collection. There is also Edmund Hillary's famous picture of Sherpa Tenzing Norgay standing for the first time on the roof of the world.

Polar exploration has also contributed significant images to the RGS library. The Society was involved in an attempt to reach the North Pole by a flotilla commanded by Captain George Nares in 1876. This yielded paintings and photographs, including fine oils hanging in the Society's lecture theatre and tea room. The most beautiful of all polar photographs, though, were by Frank Hurley, photographer of Ernest Shackleton's epic Antarctic journeys. The Society also has a superb collection of watercolours by Dr Edward Wilson, who was on Captain Robert Scott's ill-fated South Polar expedition.

Since 1830, the Royal Geographical Society has witnessed all the great moments of British exploration. The visual record of much of this thrilling saga resides in the Society's picture library, which has over the years grown steadily to its present half-million images. Its greatest treasures are collections brought back by expeditions, but many other magnificent images have come from humbler travellers showing a now-vanished world. This first-ever anthology of the cream of the Society's collection is a milestone in exploration publishing.

The peaks of the Himalayas have always exerted a magnetic pull on mountaineers, particularly its crowning jewel, Everest. An early RGS expedition team to Everest in 1922 was captured on film during a stop for breakfast by J.B. Noel.

# the world through a lens

## Michael Freeman

IN THE YEAR THE ROYAL GEOGRAPHICAL SOCIETY was founded, photography was in the process of being born. In 1826, Nicéphore Niépce, a retired French army officer, succeeded in making a permanent image of the view from his workroom window – the world's first successful photograph. It was not, however, very practical; the exposure took almost the entire day, and the pewter plate on which it was recorded was too soft for normal use.

Determined to find a way around these problems, in 1829 Niépce entered into partnership with Louis Jacques Daguerre, a theatrical designer, and the result was a workable photographic process, the daguerreotype, announced to the world in 1839. What seemed an almost magical ability to capture a scene direct from life made the new medium an instant public success.

John Ruskin, one of the pioneers of art criticism, compared a daguerreotype and a Canaletto of the same Venetian palace, and found the photograph superior: 'Every figure, crack and stain is given on a scale of an inch to Canaletto's three feet.' Although many of the comparisons made between photography and painting were naïve (Paul Delaroche declaring in 1839, 'From today, painting is dead!'), the truth was that the camera could better perform some of the roles that had to date been taken by painting and drawing. Ruskin was not handing down an aesthetic judgement. Rather he was interested in the precision of the record, and his comment highlighted what ultimately became the core strength of photography – its ability to document.

In the course of the past 150 years, photographers have experimented with many different forms and styles, and continue to do so, but the real successes of the medium have all been in reporting. Photography is at its strongest when describing the way things are.

### EARLY LIMITATIONS

In the early decades, technical and practical matters dominated photography, and it was these limitations rather than the ambitions of photographers that decided what was photographed, and in what manner. As exhibited in 1839, the daguerreotype process was hardly simple; the exposure took twenty to thirty minutes, the silvered copper plate needed to be sensitised by holding it over iodine vapour and then developed by holding it over heated mercury. The result, though it had much of the appeal of an exquisitely detailed miniature, suffered a drawback that was not immediately appreciated: the daguerreotype was a single positive image, incapable of being reproduced in multiples. This at first seemed perfectly normal. Indeed, it gave the daguerreotype a uniqueness similar to a work of art, with which early photographs were inevitably compared. Yet it was the invention of photographic negatives, from which any number of copies could be made, that transformed photography. Daguerre's process, though it was first to be invented, was a technical dead-end.

Initially, the primary demand of photographers was for portraits and outdoor scenes (the main concern for those travelling under the auspices of the Royal Geographical

Society), but both had to wait for improvements. Exposure times that had to be measured in minutes made the photography of people out of the question. Landscapes and buildings certainly had the advantage of being motionless, but all the photographic processes of the first forty years demanded on-the-spot preparation and development of the material – and in total darkness. Using a camera on location demanded heroic efforts on the part of the photographer, all the more so for those whose interests extended to parts of the planet that were difficult enough to explore without the additional burden of hauling a portable darkroom.

Looking now at the record of travel photography in the Society's archive, spanning 140 years, it is easy to overlook the physical problems that the nineteenth-century photographers faced. What seems effortless from our late twentieth-century viewpoint of foolproof photography in fact involved hardship and dedication. That there were photographers prepared to accept this reflects the appetite of the Victorian public for information and education.

The success of the British Empire, both political and economic, was enjoyed at a cultural level by its subjects at home, and there was an insatiable demand for images from afar. There was a new Victorian pragmatism in tune with the industry and the expansion of Empire, and photographs of exploration, of foreign lands and people, filled a number of needs. For one, they were a celebration of imperial success – visible evidence that British rule did indeed span the globe. They were also a catalogue of places and cultures that offered economic opportunities. And they could serve as educational images for an industrial society determined to inform itself.

## WET-PLATE PHOTOGRAPHY

The first technical revolution in photography was the invention of the wet collodion process in 1851, which reduced exposure times to between ten and ninety seconds for most outdoor subjects. Still, the attendant difficulties were formidable. Collodion was poured onto a glass plate which had to be tilted backwards and forwards until the coating was even, and the exposure needed to be made while this was still wet. The negative then had to be developed immediately. Wet-plate photography, as it was called, forced the photographer to commit himself to one worthwhile shot at a time. It left little incentive for experiment of any kind.

To begin with, this favoured what can best be called topographical photography, in which a new realism was brought to landscapes and architecture. Romantic landscape painting, with its deep vistas and overgrown ruins of ancient civilisations, was replaced by an accurate record seen through fresh eyes. In many instances, it was the earlier romantic treatment, with all the liberties that the artist took to enhance the atmosphere and mystery, which in turn inspired the new photographers to seek out the exotic.

Between 1857 and 1858, Désiré Charnay, a French schoolteacher from New Orleans, followed in the footsteps of John Lloyd Stephens and Frederick Catherwood, whose lithographs of Mayan ruins in the Mexican Yucatan served as a model of romantic exploration imagery. At around the same time, Francis Frith made three expeditions to Africa and the Middle East, travelling up the Nile to beyond the Fifth Cataract.

The images that these and other photographers were bringing back from their adventures abroad pointed out the exaggerations of illustrations that had appeared in earlier books of travel and geography, but their new realism did not necessarily mean a loss of romance. The sharp and wholly believable detail in the photographs, some of them (as in the case of Frith's) from plates as large as sixteen by twenty inches, allowed viewers to do their own exploration.

These early photographs also had the power to effect practical change. In the United States, William Henry Jackson, who had been photographing native Americans since the late 1860s, became the first person to photograph the bubbling geysers and hot springs of Yellowstone. His photographs, taken in 1871 on a U.S. Geological Survey, so impressed Congress that they played a large part in having Yellowstone created as the first national park in 1872.

Photographers who wanted to include people in their images had to pose them, and also had to persuade them to stay still. One of the earliest traveller photographers, and one of the greatest, was John Thomson, a Scot and a member of the Society. With single-minded tenacity, he spent the best part of ten years, from the late 1860s to the early '70s , travelling through Southeast Asia and China. After a first book on the newly discovered ruins at Angkor in Cambodia, he concentrated on Asian life and society, mainly in China. He worked wherever he could, in local studios, in streets and markets, building a record of a culture that was highly exotic for his Victorian audience. Thomson was one of the first ethnographic photographers, indeed one of the first reportage photographers, even if the limitations of film and equipment forced him to work in a deliberate fashion. The results were published between 1873 and 1874 in four volumes under the title *Illustrations of China and Its People*.

## DRY-PLATES AND CELLULOID

The hardships of the wet-plate photographers, sensitising and developing their images one at a time in portable dark tents, persisted for a quarter century until the invention of dry plates, which used gelatine silver bromide instead of collodion. Only after 1878 could photographers carry prepared plates for immediate use, and make exposures as short as a fraction of a second. The medium was still glass, which was hardly convenient for long periods of travel in what frequently were arduous conditions, but now photographers had the freedom to shoot without interruption.

The technical improvements in film and equipment gathered pace, stripping away, one by one, the limitations on subject matter. Photographers relished the new freedom and the chance to more fully develop their craft. A major breakthrough came in 1888, when celluloid was produced in sheets thin enough to use as a substitute for glass. A year later The Eastman Company, makers of the Kodak camera, were in production with even thinner nitro-cellulose rollfilm.

The best photographers took full advantage of these improvements, widening their range of subjects, and experimenting with original, less obvious compositions. Herbert Ponting's classic image of an ice cave is a fine example of how photographers can use the camera to explore composition, moving around a subject and searching for new viewpoints. Ponting, who was the official photographer on Scott's British Antarctic Expedition of 1910–12, was a searcher by nature. He spent three years in Japan to photograph his view of what he saw as a calm and ordered society, using a kind of minimal composition to make his point. He was one of the first to frame location scenes largely as he pleased.

## THE BEGINNINGS OF MODERN PHOTOGRAPHY

As the early years of the twentieth century unfolded, the sensitivity of film increased, and manufacturers began to produce it in rolls, on which new cameras could then expose several frames. With one loading of film, it became possible to expose several pictures one after another, without pause. All of this helped to take photography off the tripod. One of its most important effects was to democratise photography and put it in the hands of non-professionals. For expedition photography in particular, it meant that the visual record could be a straightforward adjunct to the main purpose. A professional photographer was no longer needed to document the expedition finds. Any artlessness that crept into photography because of this was offset by the greater number of pictures and a greater variety of subjects that were brought back home.

The modern era in photography began in 1926 with the introduction of the Leica, invented in Germany to use the new 35mm motion picture film stock. In comparison with anything that had gone before, this was a truly handheld, almost miniature camera, and it proved so popular and versatile that it set the standard for almost all future equipment.

Most of the developments since then have been elaborations: the single-lens reflex enabled the user to see exactly what the image would be up to the instant of exposure, and automation guaranteed the precision of exposure and focus. The single-lens reflex also made it possible to use a range of lenses of different focal length, something that was not very practical with cameras that had separate viewfinders.

Standard lenses, which had been the norm for most of photography's history, gave what was essentially the perspective of the human eye. Now there were added wide-angle lenses, which not only gave a greater angle of coverage, but if used skilfully could draw the viewer into the scene. At the other extreme, telephoto lenses magnified distant details and compressed perspective. The different focal lengths of the lenses imposed their own character on photographs.

Colour photography, which marks such a noticeable break between the older and newer images in this book, was technically feasible from the 1860s, but had to wait until 1935 and the invention of Kodachrome, a multi-layer film, to be practical for most photographers. It was not until the 1940s that colour became a real alternative to black and white, and not until the 1960s that it was the norm. To this day there are two kinds of colour photography – one in which colour film simply happens to be used, and one in which the photographer deliberately makes something of the colour qualities of the subject. The effect of the latter can be seen in a more pictorial treatment of landscapes and other outdoor scenes, with more attention than ever being paid to the sky and to subtle changes in natural lighting.

Indeed, all of the technical advances, in film, cameras and lenses, are reflected in new treatments of subjects. In many cases these are more naturalistic than was possible before. This is particularly true of ethnographic photography, an important part of the Society's collection. It could be argued that the awkwardness of some early portraits, for example, of tribal peoples, shows a kind of colonial insensitivity, and that this is in sharp contrast with a more sympathetic modern perspective in which subjects are viewed in the context of their own culture.

There is, however, a simpler explanation, and it relates to the practical side of taking photographs. Until the era of 35mm photography with its use of highly sensitive film, fast lenses and small cameras that could be used in all kinds of situations, it was hardly possible to take candid photographs of people going about their normal business. Photographing people meant posing them, and the simplest way was to face them directly. We can be fooled by the great skill of a few early photographers such as John Thomson, who directed their subjects with flair, but the fact remains that it is only in fairly modern times that photographers have been able to photograph daily life without interfering with it. Had this been possible in

the nineteenth and early twentieth centuries, we should certainly have seen more of it.

## DOCUMENTARY PHOTOGRAPHY

It is customary to view the history of photography as a series of artistic movements, but this is far from the truth. While salons and cliques tended to agonise over style, purpose and photography's place in art, the mainstream of photographers were going quietly about their work. Even within the 'artistic' history of photography, the self-conscious movements towards impressionism, symbolism, and so on have always returned, in cycles, to the documentary. In the 1890s in England this was called Naturalistic Photography; in the Germany of the 1920s it was known as New Objectivity; as 'straight' photography to Edward Weston, Paul Strand and other Americans; and so it continued. The large body of photography is continuously undergoing critical re-assessment, but as time passes the true value of documentary photography becomes more obvious. The photographers represented in the Society's archives were those who put great physical effort into their work, and it shows. They captured, with honesty and sometimes great clarity of vision, a record of places and societies as they were – frozen moments that can be studied in detail for ever.

John Thomson's photograph of the Brisbane Botanical Gardens in Australia depicts an appealing slice of life in the tropical city around 1894. Tennis players, apparently pausing for a break, pose against the backdrop of Government House and the formative stages of the exotic gardens.

Asia

# land of silk and spices

### Sir Edmund Hillary

I WAS BORN IN NEW ZEALAND and, like very many of my contemporaries, I grew up with a deep desire to travel overseas. By 1950, I had accumulated sufficient funds to make this journey. At first, although I had read many books about the Himalayas and India, I had no initial desire to go to Asia. The aim of most young New Zealanders in those days was to visit the United Kingdom and Europe and savour the traditional European culture and history, which had dominated our studies at school.

I shared a lowly six-berth cabin in a P & O liner and sailed to Britain, via the Suez Canal. In Europe, I climbed in the Austrian and Swiss Alps and then travelled in simple fashion over much of the continent.

As an antipodean, it was a remarkable experience for me to visit so many ancient historical sites. I was thrilled to see the tomb of the Black Prince in Westminster Abbey and gaped in astonishment at the Champs-Elysées and the Arc de Triomphe in Paris. I walked spellbound through the ancient ruins of Rome and the mighty Colosseum. Because there was nothing like these in New Zealand, they seemed to be the most worthwhile places to visit. I had no idea at the time that it was Asia that would soon play a very important role in my life.

Yet only a year later, in 1951, I undertook a mountaineering expedition with three other New Zealand climbers to the Gawhal area of the Himalayas. We travelled by ocean liner from Sydney to Colombo, rattled by train across Sri Lanka in a night filled with flashing fireflies. The next morning we crossed by ferry to the southern tip of India.

My limited knowledge of India told me it was a place of vast numbers of people and widespread poverty — and so initially it seemed to be. As we puffed our way north in our very modest first-class carriage we noted that the other classes were completely jammed with people. There were even hundreds of them sitting on the roof of the train. On arrival at a station they would scatter madly across the tracks, chased by policemen with bamboo batons. But when we moved on, there they were — back on the roof again.

## THE HIMALAYAS — A REVELATION

We arrived at Madras in the very early morning, and as we had some hours before the train carried on to Calcutta we walked the littered and empty streets in the dim light. At one point I noticed a thin, half-clad man lying in a gutter and assumed he was drunk. On closer examination I was shocked to realise that he was dead.

We carried on by train for hour after hour and indeed day after day — through the steamy cauldron of Calcutta and up the valley of the Ganges river. At each big station we bought hot, sweet, milky tea and meals of curry and rice. But our main impression was of heat and people — vast numbers of people, many of them poor.

The Himalayas were a revelation to us. There were masses of unclimbed peaks and no restrictions or regulations. We could go where we liked and climb anything we wanted to try. It was very different from the climbing permits and regulated areas of today.

Hong Kong, in 1857. The Chinese ceded Hong Kong island to the British in 1842, following the so-called 'Opium War'. At the time, it was considered by many to be too barren to be of much use.

As the years went by I learned far more about India. There were certainly millions of poor, but also many rich. In 1985 I was made New Zealand's High Commissioner to India and spent four-and-a-half years based in Delhi. It was an amazing time, as enormous changes were taking place. Of the 900 million people in India today more than 100 million are middle class, and even among the poor, very few people can be said to be starving. The green revolution has transformed the supply of food in this huge country.

The economic changes, too, have been vast since I made that first journey across the sub-continent. The standard of living has improved greatly and the cities are bustling with life. India still has many problems to overcome, and it will take many years to deal with them all. The people have an amazing philosophy – they do not expect change overnight, but understand that generations may have to pass before major improvements occur. But ultimately, they believe, India will become a powerful and prosperous world leader – and I am inclined to agree with them.

But to me, some of the most exciting things about India were the enormous variety of cultures and peoples; the ancient forts and palaces and temples; the wildlife parks; the rivers, lakes and coastline; and the cool hill stations.

To the north of India lies the small country of Nepal with more of the world's great mountains than anywhere else. In many ways Nepal is completely different from India. It too has a considerable variety of people, but Nepal has a unique friendliness, and practises a rather astonishing co-operation in religious and cultural matters. In contrast to India, Nepal has little mineral wealth or industrial development, and no oil of its own. It is largely self-supporting in food, and its main sources of foreign exchange are tourism and manufacturing 'Tibetan' carpets. Its superb scenery and friendly people make it very attractive to visitors.

By United Nations standards, Nepal is one of the poorest countries in the world – that is if you judge the country on its number of cars, television sets and kilometres of road per head of population. But I do not believe you can judge Nepal so easily. You have to take into account its scenic beauty, its strong religious and cultural ties, its considerable variety of food, the great cheerfulness of its people, and its remarkable community spirit.

## COMING DOWN FROM THE MOUNTAINS

I admit I am prejudiced in favour of Nepal. Its great mountains have brought me many rewards and I have worked hard with the local people to help create schools, hospitals, medical clinics, fresh water pipelines and even mountain airfields. I often think that if fate decreed that I should become an impoverished person in one of the world's poorer countries then I could think of nowhere better than in a mountain village in Nepal.

Bangladesh, to the east, is very different from both India and Nepal. Instead of high, remote mountains, it has broad, fertile river flats. Its area is half that of New Zealand (where fewer than four million people live), but it is has more than 100 million inhabitants.

A Kalmyk herdsman outside his yurt (felt tent), in the 1900s. Though their homeland is west of the Caspian Sea, Kalmyks are of Mongolian origin. Most were deported to Siberia in the 1940s.

Sadly, few countries have more natural disasters. Huge tidal waves sweep up from the Bay of Bengal and torrential floods pour down from the Himalayas. Bangladesh is frequently partly under water and the many poor living in the most vulnerable areas have a miserable existence at times. The well educated and affluent in Bangladesh have great charm and warmth, but for many people, especially women and children, life can be incredibly hard. Starvation is common, and illiteracy is widespread.

It is hard to forecast the future of Bangladesh. Women's literacy and education is of vital importance if their status is to improve, and such improvement is absolutely necessary. The population is growing fast, and some kind of family planning programme is needed. Even those, like me, who have developed a considerable affection for Bangladesh, feel a sense of desperation about its future.

## BOOMING ECONOMIES OF ASIA

In Thailand, by contrast, one finds considerable prosperity. It is a country of extensive rice fields and fast motor cars. It has spectacular temples, beautiful silk fabric, fertile flatlands threaded with canals, and dry hill areas. Its economy is booming, with growing industrialisation and increasing numbers of luxury tourist resorts and facilities.

But I have never found Thailand to be particularly friendly. As a Buddhist country, one would expect it to be generally peaceful, but in fact it is is a strange mixture of beauty combined with a solid streak of violence. An alarming number

of people die by the gun or knife – or so the media would have us believe. The country also has a reputation for dishonest policemen, substantial drug production and child prostitution, although in all honesty it must be admitted that energetic government efforts are being made to control these problems.

The extraordinary speed with which change can happen in Asia is illustrated in Thailand – and also in Singapore. Not so many years ago, this busy but yet unsophisticated little city was a place where all travellers could be sure to meet their friends in the bar of Raffles Hotel. In those days, the drains were a little on the smelly side.

What a change there has been over the last thirty or forty years! Singapore is still one of the busiest ports in the world but everything else is different. It is extraordinarily clean; magnificent high-rise buildings cover much of the island; the hotels are superb, as indeed are the shopping centres and the fine highways. Singapore's airport has to be the finest in the world and Singapore Airlines takes a bit of beating.

It is an ideal place to be in transit. With its excellent airport, hotels, taxis and well stocked shops, almost anyone can enjoy a couple of days there. It sounds like perfection and, in many ways, maybe it is.

But there are aspects of Singapore that not all of us enjoy. For a start, apart from a first-class zoo and a few similar entertainments there is a shortage of adventure activities. (Though some might say that, with so much else to do, who wants to be frightened to death anyway?) And, if you like wide open spaces, you may well find it slightly claustrophobic.

Llakpa La pass, Tibet, photographed by the explorer and naturalist Charles Howard-Bury in 1921. The picture was taken during a reconnaissance of Mount Everest.

Singapore is also an extremely disciplined place, where it is not acceptable to be critical of the Government or its laws. Some might find it too disciplined. There was a time when any young man with very long hair would not be even allowed to enter the city.

Lying just north of Singapore, there is Malaysia. In fact, the two countries were once run as one, with Malaysia being rather like Singapore's large country cousin. Malaysia's mainly Muslim population has tended to have an uneasy relationship with its minority Chinese population. As Singapore is predominantly Chinese, the association between the two countries eventually collapsed. Two years after Malaysia gained independence in 1963, Singapore seceded.

## CLIMBING HIGH

The first time I drove through Malaysia it was all rubber and palm oil plantations. In those days, Kuala Lumpur was pleasant, although not a very impressive city. But, as in Singapore, the growth and development there have been unbelievable.

I was in Kuala Lumpur again last year and what a place it is! There are huge and very attractive skyscrapers, and streets jammed with cars. I had an appointment with a television station only a couple of miles away across the city, but after being held up for two hours in a traffic jam I had to call them and cancel the arrangement.

The reason I was there was that Malaysia was planning an expedition to Mount Everest. I met the Malaysian team, who seemed fit and enthusiastic although I do not know how much climbing experience they had. The impressive thing was the money that had been raised – a million dollars from Telecom Malaysia and substantial government support.

The Prime Minister was extremely keen that young Malaysians should climb Everest, go to the North and South Poles and sail around the world. And if money counts for anything they'll probably end up doing them all.

Like Malaysia, Indonesia is undergoing expanding industrialisation and substantial economic growth – in this case, paid for by oil. Its very large population is spread over literally thousands of islands. The majority of the population is Muslim but there are many Hindus, Buddhists and Christians as well. Religious tolerance nowadays is widespread.

Indonesia is close to the equator, so rather warm, humid and fertile. It is largely volcanic in nature and it is possible to climb down into the craters of some of its sixty active volcanoes, which stretch from western Sumatra to the Lesser Sunda Islands. The island of Bali is ideal for those who want to relax in warmth and tranquillity, and the ancient Buddhist temple of Borobhodur is immensely impressive.

My first impressions of the country were of its lush beauty, but that was deceptive. Almost everyone seemed aware of political uncertainty and, indeed, violence. Later, I found that Indonesia was ruled very firmly by President Suharto and his large army. As I flew around the country, I noticed all too well the special VIP rooms for senior army officers, and how these people boarded the aircraft well ahead of the rest of us – lowly foreigners and ordinary locals.

Cars from the American Museum of Natural History's expedition in the 1920s head into the Gobi Desert in Mongolia. The expedition was the first to use motor vehicles to cross the desert.

For many years, Hong Kong has been one of the most dynamic economic centres in the region. This is apparent even before you set foot there. Some years ago, I flew into Hong Kong in an Air India jet. The Captain very kindly invited me up front for the landing and I will always remember how we came in over the city, descending until we seemed almost to be clipping the tops of the numerous skyscrapers. Ahead of us was a tiny runway pushing out into the bay – impossibly short I felt for this huge aircraft. But down we came, as smoothly as a bird, on to the runway, rolling safely to a comfortable halt.

I have always felt that the main purpose of life in Hong Kong is the making of money – huge quantities of money – and the spending of it too! The city boasts magnificent buildings, great underwater vehicular tunnels, and now the most modern airport in the world. How the political situation will develop under its new Chinese rulers nobody really knows. Certainly, some people are concerned for the future. Even in New Zealand thousands of wealthy Chinese have bought expensive houses, settled their families at school, and then returned alone to Hong Kong to make their money for as long as they can.

## THE MOST POPULOUS NATION ON EARTH

Hong Kong has been the main gateway for Chinese trade, but mainland China is itself developing a huge and vigorous economy. Although there may be much about the Chinese political system that we deplore, it is impossible to ignore almost a quarter of the world's population. Given time, changes that are certainly needed may well take place.

The Tibetan Autonomous area is one example of where change is needed. Many Tibetans have died, and they have little independence. There are now more Chinese immigrants in Tibet than local people and I have noticed much bitterness towards the Chinese in remote Tibetan villages. But still the great Chinese machine rolls on, despising foreign opinion, although at the same time rapidly developing a very foreign-like economy. Mighty leaps forward have been made in industrial development and communications - and skyscrapers have been built, too. There seems little doubt that China will become an increasingly important influence on the world economy.

Lastly, we come to Japan – one of the richest countries in the world. Its people are hard-working, determined and very talented. It is often difficult for outsiders to fully understand their culture with its strict customs and principles, and yet the media often reports the acceptance of graft at the highest levels of government. As people, they are very competitive and often replace their ancient warlike creed with challenging and dangerous sports such as extreme mountaineering.

Some years ago a senior Japanese diplomat told me, 'In our culture we only considered giving financial support to a poorer country when there was some substantial economic benefit for us. We are having to learn to give and not expect to receive.' I believe that Japan with all its wealth is indeed learning.

A Tibetan musician in the 1860s photographed by B. Simpson during a British diplomatic mission to Bhutan led by Sir Ashley Eden *(opposite)*. A proportion of Bhutan's population is ethnically Tibetan.

Huddled against the cold, four people are photographed outside their fragile bamboo home in Assam, in the far north of India *(above)*. This picture was taken in 1863 by B. Simpson, during a British diplomatic mission led by Ashley Eden to the tiny Himalayan kingdom of Bhutan. Although Bhutan was forced to cede territory to Assam in 1865, it was saved from invasion by modern India when it obtained a seat at the United Nations. Ethnically the people are Tibetan Buddhists, known as Bhutias.

A second photograph taken during the Ashley Eden mission to the Himalayan region shows a couple in front of their hut *(opposite)*. Of local people like these Eden commented: "Nothing that a Bhutia possesses is his own. He is at all times likely to lose it if it attracts the cupidity of anyone more powerful than himself. The lower classes are little better than the slaves of higher officials."

British commissioner Sir Robert Sandeman meeting the Khan of Khelat in 1867. The Khan is shown seated in the centre of the photograph, flanked by his own followers and members of the British party. The territory over which the Khan ruled was in Baluchistan, southwestern Pakistan, between India and Afghanistan. Captain Sandeman succeeded in persuading the Baluchi tribesmen to end their insurgency against the Khan, who in gratitude leased the land around the strategic Bolan Pass into Afghanistan to British India.

Another picture from the 1860s shows the Durbar (meeting house) and temples in Kathmandu, Nepal. The photograph, by Captain Taylor, shows a Nepalese military commander, General Shamshere, and his entourage. The mountainous kingdom of Nepal lies high in the Himalayas, between India and Tibet. As the temples in the picture suggest, its people are mainly Hindus. Nepal remained independent throughout British rule in neighbouring India.

Two dacoits or robbers, crucified by villagers for their crimes in Burma (Myanmar) in the 1880s *(above)*. This form of execution was common in nineteenth-century Burma, especially north of the capital, Mandalay. In some cases, victims were killed before being lashed to a frame of the kind shown here; in others they were merely wounded and left to die.

Gholam Mortiza Khan, chief of the Bugti clan from central Pakistan, with his sons *(opposite)*, photographed by F. Bremner of Karachi, probably in the 1860s or 70s. The Bugti were fine warriors and horsemen, and were also hereditary robbers, a role of which they were proud.

Benares – now also known as Varanasi – in the 1890s. This Hindu place of pilgrimage, on the banks of the River Ganges in India, was photographed in the 1890s by John Thomson. The burning wood smoke in the centre of the foreground is a reminder that it was, and still is, traditional for Hindus to cremate the dead. Even when the cremation takes place elsewhere, the relations of the dead person may travel long distances to scatter the ashes on the sacred River Ganges.

Rubber trees in Sri Lanka in the 1880s. At this time, rubber was a relatively new plantation crop in the country then known as Ceylon. Since the 1840s, coffee had been the only crop grown on a large scale, but the crop failed in the 1870s and plantation owners decided to diversify into tea and rubber. These crops remain the mainstay of Sri Lanka's economy.

Stone dwellings cling to the hillside in Dunkar, in the Spiti valley in northern India. Spiti lies at an altitude of 2750 metres (9022 feet) in the Himalayas. This photograph, taken by Francis Frith in the 1870s, shows the harsh terrain and climate of the region: a glacier is visible in the valley beyond the settlement.

A woman of Sikkim carrying firewood, photographed by Messrs Johnston and Hoffman of Darjeeling in the 1890s *(opposite)*. Sikkim is a Himalayan region of north India that borders on Nepal, Bhutan and Tibet. The people of Sikkim were Buddhists, but by the time this photo was taken, many Hindus had emigrated from Nepal.

European children in Fukien (now called Fujian), China, with their servant in the mid-1890s *(above)*. This photograph was taken by Mrs Isabella Bishop, who travelled extensively in the region. Although these children seem strong and healthy, Mrs Bishop was not always optimistic about the advisability of bringing up European children in Asia. She reported that in French Cochinchina (now part of Vietnam) the incidence of disease was so high that they could not survive.

The village of Tindi, in Daghestan, in the late 1890s *(opposite)*. This region of the southern Caucasus is home to a mixed population, many of whom are Muslims (a mosque can be seen to the left of the village). The photograph was taken by M. de Déchy, who returned from the area with large collections of plants, fossils and photographs.

A bullock cart, photographed by John Thomson in India in the 1890s *(above)*. The wheels of the cart and the bullocks' horns are painted in decorative colours – a custom which continues today. The bullocks are long-horned, humped-backed zebu cattle which are still common throughout Africa and Asia. They were considered sacred in India.

A group of Ainu people from Japan, photographed by Professor J. Milne in 1892. Behind the group is a hedge of prayer sticks called *inau*, made from carefully whittled willow wands. This was traditionally set up to the east of each hut in a village, along with the skulls of animals killed in hunting. The Ainu, who have lived in the north of Japan and its neighbouring islands for thousands of years, are both physically and culturally very different from the rest of the population of Japan.

Five magnificently dressed lay-lamas, photographed in Sikkim in the 1890s by Messrs Johnston and Hoffman of Darjeeling. Lamas are Buddhist monks or teachers in the Tibetan tradition and occupy such a significant part in the religion that it used to be known as 'lamaism'. The population of Sikkim was largely Buddhist at the time of this photo, although waves of immigrants from Indian and Nepal later brought Hinduism with them.

Men carrying tea in Sichuan, China, photographed by E.H. Wilson in 1908 *(opposite)*. The tea, packed into bricks, was destined for neighbouring Tibet. Wilson reported that a single load might weigh as much as 143 kilograms (317 pounds) and that the men might carry this as far as 9 kilometres (6 miles) a day 'over vile roads'.

Crowds make their way along Queen's Road Central, Hong Kong *(above left)*. Queen's Road was built early in Hong Kong's history, and from the beginning the Central area was earmarked for Chinese traders. This photograph was taken by R.C. Hurley in 1897.

A second photograph from Hong Kong, of the same date, also taken by R.C. Hurley, shows the Happy Valley racecourse *(above right)*. Racing has always been popular in Hong Kong. The horses used when this picture was taken were tough, small animals from Mongolia, known at the time as China ponies. Today, conventional racehorses are used.

Tibetan Buddhists in the early 1880s pose for the camera, dressed for a traditional dance. This photograph was taken by Sarat Chandra Das, a member of the Education Department of India, who made what was at the time a hazardous and rarely accomplished visit to Lhasa, the capital of Tibet, as part of his research into the Tibetan language. He published an account of his travels, in English, in 1902.

A group of nuns, photographed by John Claude White at a Tibetan nunnery, in the early 1900s. Tibetans are traditionally very devout and before the Chinese takeover of the country and the exile of the Dalai Lama in the 1950s, about twenty percent of young men were monks. Nuns, or *anis*, were always fewer in number, and were sometimes under the supervision of monks.

The Great Wall of China, in 1907, as photographed by Herbert Ponting. Over the centuries, there had been a number of attempts to build some sort of fortification or earthworks along this route, but the wall that appears here was built during the Ming Dynasty (1368–1644). It remains the world's longest manmade structure.

According to Herbert Ponting, who took this photograph in 1907, this is 'a fakir in Benares' (Varanasi), India. Strictly speaking, a fakir is a Muslim religious mendicant, but here Ponting is referring to a Hindu holy man. He is a yogi, or one who practises yoga and has perfected the control of mind over body to such an extent that he can withstand the physical pain of the bed of nails on which he is sitting.

Jaipur in 1900, photographed by John Thomson. Jaipur is capital of the
Indian state of Rajasthan and is famous for its magnificent, pink sandstone
buildings. One particularly famous landmark, the city palace complex
dominates this picture. The tall structure at the front of it is the 'Palace of
the Winds', built in 1799. Although a dramatic sight when viewed head on,
it is in fact little more than a facade.

A falconer to the Wang of Hami in Xinjiang (formerly Sinkiang), China, with a golden eagle *(opposite)*. This photograph was taken by Douglas Carruthers during an expedition into Central Asia between 1910 and 1911. The Wang was a traditional Islamic ruler in this part of China which, bordering on Mongolia is, as Carruthers described it, 'on the threshold of the Moslem and the Buddhist worlds'.

A Khalkh woman from the northern Gobi desert in Mongolia demonstrates her complex, traditional hairstyle *(above)*. Her elaborate jewellery and hair ornaments are made of silver and turquoise. The Khalkh are the largest ethnic group in Mongolia. This photograph was also taken in 1910–11 by Douglas Carruthers.

A group of Victorian travellers gazes out across the tranquil landscape from The Pilgrim's Rest, at the foot of the Schwedagon pagoda, near Rangoon in Burma. The pagoda is one of the most revered in Burma, possibly in the whole of Southeast Asia, and is surrounded by rest-houses for pilgrims and numerous smaller pagodas. This photograph was taken in 1900, by V. C. Scott O'Connor.

A memorial arch, decorated with carved dragons *(opposite)*. This magnificent structure, built in memory of a virtuous widow, was photographed in Sichuan province, western China, in 1908 by the British naturalist, E. H. Wilson. Wilson noticed that such memorials were 'a common wayside feature in the west'.

The Potala, the former palace of the Dalai Lama, in Lhasa, Tibet *(above)*. This spectacular gold-roofed building, with over 1000 rooms, used to house both the Dalai Lama and a community of monks, but is now a museum. The photograph was taken by Captain C. G. Rawlings in 1904, part of an expedition led by Sir Francis Younghusband, later president of the RGS. They were the first Europeans to see the holy city.

A cane suspension bridge, built by the Arbor people of Assam in northeast India, spans the River Dihang *(above)*. Photographed on an expedition led by A. Bentinck in 1911, it was considered a particularly fine example of this kind of traditional bridge. It was made from a cage of interlacing canes, supported by being lashed with cane and creepers to posts on the river banks. It was 240 metres (786 feet) long and swung 15 metres (50 feet) above the water.

A Burmese boatman, photographed in 1910 by V.C. Scott O'Connor, sits alone in the stern of his barge *(opposite)*. Although magnificently decorated, these boats were used for carrying goods, principally palm oil. Most were based at the town of Yenangyaung on the Irrawaddy River. The boatmen moved their craft along by punting them through shallow water.

Bactrian camels, photographed in Xinjiang in 1910–11 by Douglas Carruthers *(opposite)*. These two-humped camels, used in the Gobi (where a few still live wild) and other desert regions of Central Asia, are closely related to the dromedaries of Arabia, and like them are able to survive for long periods without food or water. They have longer hair than dromedaries, and so are better able to withstand extremes of heat and cold.

A woman with reindeer in the Upper Yenesi Basin in Mongolia *(above)*. The people of this densely forested region depended on reindeer as riding animals, for carrying baggage, and to supply skins for clothing. Douglas Carruthers, who photographed the woman during his 1910–11 expedition, noticed that it was the practice to clip the animals' antlers, to help them make their way among the trees.

The valley of Tsagaan Nuur, Mongolia, photographed in 1925, during the
American Museum of Natural History expedition to Mongolia. A wind-
eroded escarpment is visible in the distance, about 24 kilometres (15 miles)
away, between which and a lake beyond it was an area of shifting sand
dunes. The expedition had set out to investigate the theory that
mammalian life originated in Mongolia. Instead of finding evidence to
support this theory, they discovered huge numbers of dinosaur fossils.

The Lower Remo Glacier, Kashmir, photographed by Dr Filippo de Filippa in around 1915. The remarkable landscape of ice needles and pinnacles illustrates the dramatic effects of a glacier. Compacted snow and ice build up to form a river of ice. At the lower end of the glacier the ice melts, creating a clear stream or lake.

A Tibetan family, dressed in their finest traditional clothes, photographed by Alexander Wollaston in 1921 *(above)* on an early attempt to climb Mount Everest, organised by the Alpine Club and the RGS.

This picture *(opposite)* shows a Tibetan dancing girl and was taken by Captain J.B. Noel in 1922. Captain Noel was a photographer who travelled extensively in the Himalayas. In addition to recording local costume and traditions in still photographs such as that shown here, he was also a pioneer of moving pictures and filmed a number of dances and other ceremonies using 'kinematograph'.

The Tsangpo River in Tibet flows through a spectacular gorge *(opposite)*. This photograph was taken in 1924 by the British botanist Frank Kingdon-Ward, who travelled through the valley of the Tsangpo (now called the Yarlung Zangbo) in search of the river's source. He found the valley rich in plant life, and sent 250 specimens back to Britain. When the Yarlung Zangpo leaves Tibet and enters India it becomes the Brahamaputra.

Bactrian camels cross sand dunes at Tsagaan Nuur, Mongolia, in 1925 *(above)*. They belonged to the expedition from the American Museum of Natural History, whose fleet of cars is shown on page 24. The 125 camels were used for sending supplies, including petrol, ahead of the vehicles. The belt of dunes shown here is over 160 kilometres (100 miles) long, though only about 5 kilometres (3 miles) wide.

Whipping boys, complete with whips, rest in the sunshine in an undated photograph by Douglas Carruthers *(above)*. The boys were attached to an official Chinese retinue. Carruthers' travels in Xinjiang, in eastern China, brought him into contact with the traditional ruler of the area, the Wang of Hami, who in turn owed allegiance to the Emperor of China.

A boy in the eastern Himalayas, carrying a young child on his back *(opposite)*. Like children all over the developing world today, he is expected to be responsible for younger siblings. This photograph was taken by Frank Kingdon-Ward, who travelled to this region in 1935, retracing much of his earlier trip along the Tsangpo.

A Maru girl, dressed in boots and traditional jewellery, poses for the camera while sitting in a mountain stream *(opposite)*. This photograph by Frank Kingdon-Ward was taken on a visit to the Assam-Burma border area in the late 1930s.

A Naga woman from Burma, also photographed by Frank Kingdon-Ward in the late 1930s *(above left)*. The Naga people live mainly in Assam in India, though a significant number live on the Burmese side of the border. The outside world had paid little attention to the Naga until World War II, when they helped British-led forces defeat Japanese troops in their region.

A young monk, photographed in Tibet by Frank Kingdon-Ward in 1933 *(above right)*. He carries a prayer wheel in one hand, and a rosary in the other. In the Tibetan form of Buddhism, a boy may enter a monastery at the age of eleven, when he takes a series of vows, followed by many years of hard study and meditation.

The base camp during a 1922 expedition to Everest, photographed by Captain J. B. Noel. Noel had been on a trip to Everest the year before and had filmed part of the journey. This earlier expedition was for reconnaissance purposes, and was the first to obtain permission to approach the mountain from the Tibetan side.

The Valley of Dzag in central Mongolia, photographed by Paul Harris *(opposite)*. The valley, at the eastern end of the Hangayn mountains, is a summer pasture for yaks, horses and sheep and is also used as a staging area for herds being brought down from pastures higher in the Hangayn.

The Brunei Rainforest Project area *(above left),* also photographed by Paul Harris. This project was a scientific expedition run jointly during 1991/2 by the Royal Geographical Society and the University of Brunei Darussalam to study the rainforest in the Temburong district of Brunei. Scientists from Europe and Asia worked with local people, studying plant ecology, hydrology and the insect, reptile and mammal species.

A fishing boat in full sail drifts on the calm waters of a lagoon in Kerala state, south India, photographed by Maurice Joseph *(above right)*. Fishing is an important industry in this picturesque, but poor and densely populated part of the Malabar coast.

Sherpa Tenzing Norgay, photographed at 11.30 a.m. on 29 May, 1953, by Edmund Hillary at the moment the pair became the first people to reach the summit of Everest *(opposite)*. The two were members of a British team led by John Hunt. Everest's enormous height of 8848 metres (29,028 feet) above sea level means that the atmosphere near the summit is very thin, so Hillary and Tenzing carried oxygen supplies with them. Tenzing's oxygen mask is clearly visible. Without oxygen-breathing apparatus, developed during World War II, the ascent would not have been possible.

Hillary and Tenzing drink a celebratory cup of tea at the camp on West Cwm, after their successful assault on Everest's summit in May 1953 *(above)*. The photograph, taken by George Band, shows them wearing the insulated boots and other special clothing used for the expedition.

A man and his donkey make their way across a precarious bridge over a rushing mountain torrent in the Chitral valley in Pakistan, photographed by Steve Razzetti. Hemmed in by the massive mountains of the Hindu Kush and the Hindu Raj, this part of Pakistan is almost cut off from the outside world, many places being, as this picture indicates, impossible to reach by any means other than on foot.

The Khumbi Himal, within the Sagarmartha National Park, Nepal, photographed by Paul Harris from Gokyo Ri, a 5500 metre (18,000 feet) peak. Gokyo Lake lies in the centre of the picture; beyond it lies the massive boulder-strewn Ngozumba Glacier. Mount Everest itself is not visible in this photograph, although it can be seen from where it was taken, along with three other mountains that are over 8000 metres (26,200 feet) high. This area is the home of Nepal's Sherpa communities.

Tibetan prayer flags at Leh Gompah monastery in the Ladakh mountains of Jammu and Kashmir, India, photographed by Ian Cumming. The people here are largely Buddhist, in the Tibetan tradition. Prayer flags such as these, many with mantras (special words or sounds used in meditation) written on them, can be seen at shrines and monasteries throughout the Ladakh region.

A village high in the Zanskar mountains of Jammu and Kashmir looks out over a wide green valley. The floor of the valley, formed by retreating glaciers, is dotted with boulders left behind by melting ice and criss-crossed by mountain streams. This photograph by Ian Cumming was taken at the very end of the summer.

An eagle hunter in Bayan Olgei Province, Mongolia, photographed in 1990 by Paul Harris. This part of Mongolia is adjacent to Kazakhstan, and many of the people living there, like this hunter, are Kazakhs. Training eagles to hunt is a tradition in Central Asia. The eagles are caught in the wild and trained throughout the summer. In winter they are used to hunt small mammals such as marmots. Mature eagles have a wingspan of up to 2.5m (8 feet) and have been known to attack a snow leopard.

Building a yurt (locally known as a *ger*) in Mongolia, photographed by Paul Harris *(opposite)*. A lattice framework about 3 metres (about 11.5 feet) in diameter is covered with layers of felt and canvas. The whole process of erecting a yurt takes between one and two hours. These tents are the main form of housing in rural Mongolia – and even form small shanties on the outskirts of larger cities. In the past, the components would have been carried by camel, but today, small trucks are often used.

Fishermen wait patiently, perched high on stilts above the incoming tide, photographed by Chris Caldicott on the southwest coast of Sri Lanka *(above)*. The stilts used in this traditional style of fishing are fixed permanently in position. The fishermen climb them and cast from their rods into the sea as the tide drives the fish towards them. The fisherman in the foreground is an old man brought up in the tradition of fishing in this way – a tradition that is gradually disappearing.

Horse-herders returning home after a horse festival near Karakorum, the ancient capital of Genghis Khan's Mongolian empire. This photograph by Paul Harris shows the herders at sunset. The festival itself involves horse-racing for boys under twelve years old, as well as wrestling and archery competitions. All these skills are important to Mongolians, and were highly valued by their ancestors, who made up Genghis Khan's army.

A lama at early morning prayer at the Gandan monastery, in Mongolia, photographed by Paul Harris. Buddhism in Mongolia follows the Tibetan tradition. Communist persecution in the 1930s and 40s drove the religion almost to extinction, but it has revived recently. Gandan itself has been important in re-establishing the Buddhist faith in Mongolia and many of the 700 monasteries once destroyed are now being rebuilt.

A carving on the wall of the Hindu temple Pura Rambat Siwi on the west coast of Bali, Indonesia, photographed by David Constantine *(above left)*. The temple was built in honour of the sea and is close to a group of sacred caves. Bali is famous for its extraordinary number of temples, and clings to its Hindu faith in the midst of Islamic Indonesia.

A delightful bas relief on the Pura Madwe Karang, at Kubutmbahan in Bali, photographed in 1992 by Chris Caldicott *(above right)*. It shows a temple official riding a bicycle made up of flowers and petals. The temple honours the earth and the sun, and ceremonies take place here to bless crops such as coffee that grow on unirrigated land.

The mountains of central Sri Lanka, photographed by Chris Caldicott *(opposite)*. The beautiful hill country is wooded, with grassy uplands. Slightly lower down the mountains there are tea plantations, but at this point the climate is too cool, with a risk of frost.

Children in Shekawati, in the state of Rajasthan, India, photographed by Chris Caldicott *(above)*. This desert area was once a route for merchants travelling between Asia and Europe, and local landowners grew wealthy from charging tolls. With the proceeds, they built ornate buildings called *havelis*, many of which now lie neglected. The children here are in the doorway of one such building.

Elephants photographed in 1996 by Chris Caldicott, being washed in the Gandak River, at Sonepur Mela, in Bihar, India *(opposite)*. The Gandak flows into the sacred River Ganges at this point. Every November, during a time of pilgrimage, the biggest elephant market in the world takes place here, part of the Sonepur Mela livestock fair. Up to 300 elephants may be sold at the fair, and each must be washed in the river, morning and evening.

Rice fields near Padangkerta, Bali, with the volcano Gunung Agung in the background, photographed by Michael Freeman. Rice is Bali's most important crop, growing well in the rich volcanic soil. It is planted in terraced paddy fields and quickly sends up green shoots. When ripe, it is golden brown and almost everyone in the neighbourhood joins in the harvest, cutting the stalks, removing the husks and storing the grain.

Caught in a shaft of sunlight, a trader sells red-skinned onions in the huge
covered vegetable market in Ahmedabad, India *(above left)*. Ahmedabad is
the capital of Gujarat, a state where most people are vegetarian. The
photograph was taken by David Constantine.

A nomad woman of Tibet shows off her jewellery, photographed by
Norma Joseph *(above right)*. Tibetans love ornaments: this woman's hair is
decorated with beads of silver, turquoise, coral and amber and she wears
beads around her neck, as well as an amulet. Both men and women wear
earrings – though men prefer to wear just one.

A man with a sewing machine, photographed by David Constantine, plies
his trade in the streets of Pokhara in Nepal *(opposite)*. Working outside has
the advantage of advertising the tailor's work.

Africa

# the dark continent

## Dr. Richard Leakey

THE CONCEPT OF AFRICAN EXPLORATION has been greatly influenced by the hero status given to the European adventurers and missionaries who went off to Africa in the last century. Their travels and travails were certainly extraordinary and nobody can help but be impressed by the tremendous physical and intellectual courage that was so much a characteristic of people such as Livingstone, Stanley, Speke and Baker, to name just a few. The challenges and rewards that Africa offered, both in terms of commerce and also 'saved souls', inspired people to take incredible risks and endure personal suffering to a degree that was probably unique to the exploration of Africa.

I myself am fortunate enough to have had the opportunity to organise one or two minor expeditions to remote spots in Africa where there were no roads or airfields and marching with porters and/or camels was the best option at the time. I have also had the thrill of being with people untouched and often unmoved by contact with Western or other technologically based cultures and these experiences remain for me amongst the most exciting and salutary of my life. With the contemporary revolution in technology, there will be few if any such opportunities again. Indeed I often find myself slightly saddened by the realisation that were life ever discovered on another planet, exploration would doubtless be done by remote sensing and making full use of artificial, digital intelligence. At least it is unlikely to be in my lifetime and this is a relief!

Notwithstanding all of this, I believe that the age of exploration and discovery in Africa is far from over. The future offers incredible opportunities for new discoveries that will push back the frontiers of knowledge. This endeavour will of course not involve exotic and arduous journeys into malaria-infested tropical swamps, but it will certainly require dedication, team work, public support and a conviction that the rewards to be gained will more than justify the efforts and investment.

### EARLY EXPLORERS

Let me start with some thoughts about Africa and the Royal Geographical Society's commitment to African exploration. Many of us were raised and educated at school with the belief that Africa, the so-called 'Dark Continent', was actually *discovered* by early European travellers and explorers. The date of this 'discovery' is difficult to establish, and anyway a distinction has always had to be drawn between northern Africa and the vast area south of the Sahara. The Romans certainly had information about the continent's interior as did others such as the Greeks. A diverse range of traders ventured down both the west coast and the east coast from at least the ninth century, and by the tenth century Islam had taken root in a number of new towns and settlements established by Persian and Arab interests along the eastern tropical shores. Trans-African trade was probably under way well before this time, perhaps partly stimulated by external interests.

Close to the beginning of the first millenium, early Christians were establishing the Coptic Church in the ancient kingdom of Ethiopia and at other coastal settlements along Africa's northern Mediterranean coast. Along the west coast of Africa, European trade in gold, ivory and people was well

The British camp at Senafe, Abyssinia (now Ethiopia), in about 1868. The year before, a large British force under General Sir Robert Napier was sent into Ethiopia to rescue the British consul and some missionaries held prisoner by Emperor Theodore. Napier defeated the Ethiopians at Magdala in 1868, and the Emperor shot himself.

established by the sixteenth century. Several hundred years later, early in the nineteenth century, the systematic penetration and geographical exploration of Africa was undertaken by Europeans, seeking geographical knowledge and territory, and looking for opportunities not only for commerce but for the chance to spread the Gospel.

The extraordinary narratives of some of the journeys of early European travellers and adventurers in Africa are a vivid reminder of just how recently Africa has become embroiled in the power struggles and vested interests of non-Africans.

## AFRICA'S GIFT TO THE WORLD

My own preoccupation over the past thirty years has been to study human prehistory, and from this perspective it is very clear that Africa was never 'discovered' in the sense in which so many people have been and, perhaps, still are being taught. Rather, it was Africans themselves who found that there was a world beyond their shores.

Prior to about two million years ago, the only humans or proto-humans in existence were confined to Africa; as yet, the remaining world had not been exposed to this strange mammalian species which in time came to dominate the entire planet. It is no trivial matter to recognise the cultural implications that arise from this entirely different perspective of Africa and its relationship to the rest of humanity.

How many of the world's population grow up knowing that it was in fact *African* people who first moved and settled in southern Europe, Central Asia and migrated to the Far East?

How many know that Africa's principle contribution to the world is in fact humanity itself? These concepts are quite different from the notion that Africa was only 'discovered' in the past few hundred years, and will surely change the commonly held idea that somehow Africa is a 'laggard', late to come onto the world stage.

It could be argued that our early human forebears – the *Homo erectus* who moved out of Africa – have little or no bearing on the contemporary world and its problems. I disagree, and believe that the often pejorative thoughts that are associated with the 'Dark Continent' and dark skins, as well as with the general sense that Africans are somehow outside the mainstream of human achievement, would be entirely negated by the full acceptance of a universal African heritage for all of humanity. This, after all, is the truth that has now been firmly established by scientific inquiry.

The study of human origins and prehistory will surely continue to be important in a number of regions of Africa and this research must continue to rank high on the list of relevant ongoing exploration and discovery. There is still much to be learned about the early stages of human development, and the age of the 'first humans' – the first bipedal apes – has not been firmly established. The current hypothesis is that prior to five million years ago there were no bipeds, and this would mean that humankind is only five million years old. Beyond Africa, there were no humans until just two million years ago, and this is a consideration which political leaders and people as a whole need to bear in mind.

Cape Town, as it was c. 1917. Trade first brought Europeans to these shores – first the Portuguese Ruiz Bartolomé
(Bartholomew Diaz) in 1487, searching for a sea route to the East, and later Jan van Riebeeck in 1652,
who established a supply post here for Dutch ships.

## RECENT HISTORY

When it comes to the relatively recent history of Africa's
contemporary people, there is still considerable ignorance. The
evidence suggests that there were major migrations of people
within the continent during the past 5000 years, and the impact
of the introduction of domestic stock must have been quite
considerable on the way of life of many of Africa's people. Early
settlements and the beginnings of nation states are, as yet, poorly
researched and recorded. Although archaeological studies have
been undertaken in Africa for well over a hundred years, there
remain more questions than answers.

One question of universal interest concerns the origin
and inspiration for the civilisation of early Egypt. The Nile has,
of course, offered opportunities for contacts between the heart
of Africa and the Mediterranean sea coast but very little is
known about human settlement and civilisation in the upper
reaches of the Blue and White Nile between 4000 and 10,000
years ago. We do know that the present Sahara Desert is only
about 10,000 years old; before this Central Africa was wetter and
more fertile, and research findings have shown that it was only
during the past 10,000 years that Lake Turkana in northern
Kenya was isolated from the Nile system. When connected, it
would have been an excellent connection between the heartland
of the continent and the Mediterranean.

Another question focuses on the extensive stone-walled
villages and towns in Southern Africa. The Great Zimbabwe is
but one of thousands of standing monuments in East, Central
and Southern Africa which attest to considerable human

endeavour in Africa long before contact with Europe or Arabia.
The Neolithic period and Iron Age still offer very great
opportunities for exploration and discovery.

As an example of the importance of history, let us look
at the modern South Africa where a visitor might still be struck
by the not-too-subtle representation of a past which, until a few
years ago, only 'began' with the arrival of Dutch settlers some
400 years back. There are, of course, many pre-Dutch sites
including extensive fortified towns where kingdoms and nation
states had thrived hundreds of years before contact with Europe,
but this evidence has been poorly documented and even more
poorly portrayed.

Few need to be reminded of the sparseness of Africa's
pre-colonial written history. There are countless cultures and
historical narratives that have never been recorded except as oral
history and legend. As post-colonial Africa further consolidates
itself, history must be reviewed and deepened to incorporate the
realities of precolonial human settlement as well as foreign
contact. Africa's identity and self-respect is closely linked to this.

One of the great tragedies is that African history was
of little interest to the early European travellers who were in a
hurry and had no brief to document the details of the people
that they came across during their travels. In the basements
of countless European museums, there are stacked shelves of
African 'curios' – objects taken from the people but seldom
documented in terms of the objects' use, customs and history.

There is surely an opportunity here for contemporary
scholars to do something. While much of Africa's pre-colonial

Extremes of weather can have a powerful effect on the South African landscape, torrential rain after drought turning areas of near-desert into carpets of flowers. Here, in a photograph taken in the Cape Province in around 1920, a recently flooded mud flat has been turned into a crazy pattern of cracks and fissures by the fierce African sun.

past has been obscured by the slave trade, colonialism, evangelism and modernisation, there remains an opportunity, at least in some parts of the continent, to record what still exists. This has to be one of the most vital frontiers for African exploration and discovery as we approach the end of this millenium. Some of the work will require trips to the field but great gains could be achieved by a systematic and coordinated effort to record the inventories of European museums and archives. The Royal Geographical Society could well play a leading role in this chapter of African exploration. The compilation of a central data bank on what is known and what exists would, if based on a coordinated initiative to record the customs and social organisation of Africa's remaining indigenous peoples, be a huge contribution to the heritage of mankind.

## MEDICINES AND FOODS

On the African continent itself, there remain countless other areas for exploration and discovery. Such endeavours will be achieved without the fanfare of great expeditions and high adventure as was the case during the last century and they should, as far as possible, involve exploration and discovery of African frontiers by Africans themselves. These frontiers are not geographical: they are boundaries of knowledge in the sphere of Africa's home-grown cultures and natural world.

Indigenous knowledge is a very poorly documented subject in many parts of the world and Africa is a prime example of a continent where centuries of accumulated local knowledge is rapidly disappearing in the face of modernisation. I believe, for

example, that there is much to be learned about the use of wild African plants for both medicinal and nutritional purposes. Such knowledge, kept to a large extent as the experience and memory of elders in various indigenous communities, could potentially have far-reaching benefits for Africa and for humanity as a whole.

The importance of new remedies based on age-old medicines cannot be underestimated. Over the past two decades, international companies have begun to take note and to exploit certain African plants for pharmacological preparations. All too often, Africa has not been the beneficiary of these 'discoveries' which are, in most instances, nothing more than the refinement and improvement of traditional African medicine. The opportunities for exploration and discovery in this area are immense and will have assured economic return on investment. One can only hope that such work will be in partnership with the people of Africa and not at the expense of the continent's best interests.

Within the same context, there is much to be learned about the traditional knowledge of the thousands of plants that have been utilised by different African communities for food. The contemporary world has become almost entirely dependent, in terms of staple foods, on the cultivation of only six principle plants: corn, wheat, rice, yams, potatoes and bananas. This cannot be a secure basis to guarantee the food requirements of more than five billion people.

Many traditional food plants in Africa are drought-resistant and might well offer new alternatives for large-scale

An undated photograph of the diamond-mining boom town of Kimberley, South Africa. In 1870, diamonds were discovered below ground in the 'dry diggings' in and around Kimberley. By 1871, up to 75,000 men of all colours had flocked to the diamond fields, including the Briton Cecil Rhodes who made his fortune in diamonds.

agricultural development in the years to come. Crucial to this development is finding out what African people used before exotics were introduced. In some rural areas of the continent, it is still possible to learn about much of this by talking to the older generation. It is certainly a great shame that some of the early European travellers in Africa were ill-equipped to study and record details of diet and traditional plant use, but I am sure that, whilst it is late, it is not too late. The compilation of a pan-African data base on what is known about the use of the continent's plant resources is a vital matter requiring action.

## VANISHING SPECIES

In the same spirit, there is as yet a very incomplete inventory of the continent's other species. The inevitable trend of bringing land into productive management is resulting in the loss of unknown but undoubtedly large numbers of species. This genetic resource may be invaluable to the future of Africa and indeed humankind, and there really is a need for coordinated efforts to record and understand the continent's biodiversity.

In recent years important advances have been made in the study of tropical ecosystems in Central and South America, and I am sure that similar endeavours in Africa would be rewarding. At present, Africa's semi-arid and highland ecosystems are better understood than the more diverse and complex lowland forests, which are themselves under particular threat from loggers and farmers. The challenges of exploring the biodiversity of the upper canopy in the tropical forests, using the same techniques that are now used in Central American forests,

are fantastic and might also lead to eco-tourist developments for these areas in the future.

It is indeed an irony that huge amounts of money are being spent by the advanced nations in an effort to discover life beyond our own planet, whilst at the same time nobody on this planet knows the extent and variety of life here at home. The tropics are especially relevant in this regard and one can only hope that Africa will become the focus of renewed efforts of research on bio-diversity and tropical ecology.

## AN AFROCENTRIC VIEW

Overall, the history of Africa has been presented from an entirely Eurocentric or even Caucasocentric perspective, and until recently this has not been adequately reviewed. The penetration of Africa, especially during the last century, was important in its own way, but today the realities of African history, art, culture and politics are better known. The time has come to regard African history in terms of what has happened in Africa itself, rather than simply in terms of what non-African individuals did when they first travelled to the continent.

Two rare and very early pictures *(opposite)*, taken by the Scottish explorer Colonel James Augustus Grant in 1860. On their 1860-63 expedition, Grant and John Speke found the source of the Nile, and together they also took some of the earliest pictures of Zanzibar. The first photograph *(above)* shows a slave market in Zanzibar, with a row of female slaves just visible in the shadows on the right. The second picture *(below)* is inscribed '"Wanyamweris" or natives from the Country of the Moon'. The men have a moon-shaped patch of hair on their heads.

*Slave Market-place, Zanzibar - very difficult to take - slaves & arabs kept running away leaving only a line of women slaves whose legs and a face or two may be observed - the women's entire dress is a blue cotton sheet or cloth tied tight under arms and extending as far as the knee-their heads are cropped as close as scizzors can crop them - very often they have for ornament a hole through the upper lip - at the market they come out very clean - Houses are blocks of coralline partly plastered - an indistinct wily arab squats to the right eyeing the women*

Nº 7

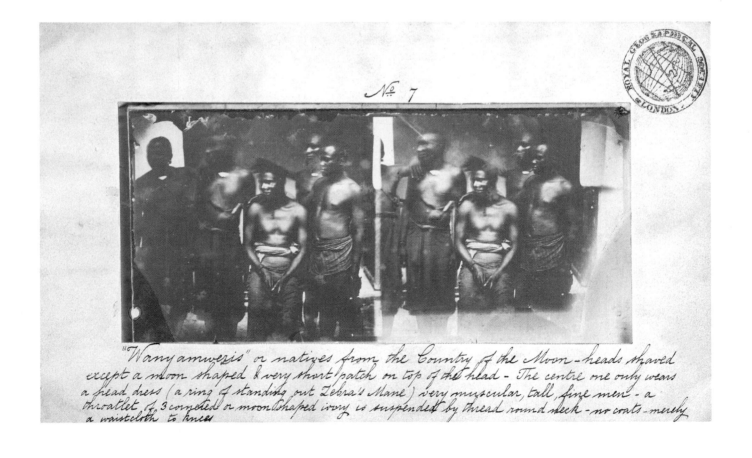

*"Wanyamwezis" or natives from the Country of the Moon - heads shaved except a moon shaped & very short patch on top of the head - The centre one only wears a head dress (a ring of standing out Zebra's Mane) very muscular, tall, fine men - a throatlet of 3 cornered or moon shaped ivory is suspended by thread round neck - no coats - merely a waistcloth to knees*

An ox, a camel and their handlers stand ankle-deep in the floodwaters of the Nile, in a photograph taken in the 1860s by Mrs. G. Lekegian. Travel to the Nile burgeoned in the years following 1869 – in the name of tourism rather than exploration – with the establishment of Thomas Cook & Son's Egypt office in Cairo, and the opening of the Suez canal, which brought visitors to Egypt on their way to India.

A barefoot Egyptian water carrier mounts stone steps with a water-filled animal skin on his back *(above left)*, and *(above right)* a beautifully composed photograph contains all the classic elements associated with Egypt – camels, palm trees, Nile waters, and behind them all, three pyramids. Prints of such early 'tourist' views of Egypt would have been available for sale. Like the photograph opposite, these scenes were taken by Mrs Lekegian in the 1860s. At this point photography was in its infancy, being only about twenty years old. What makes these pictures remarkable is both their great age, and the way in which the photographer has clearly seen and exploited the artistic potential of the new medium.

A group of European tourists with their guides visit the Great Sphinx at Giza in Egypt, in about 1867. With its leonine body and human face, the statue was carved in the likeness of King Kephren whose pyramid it guards. The correct name of the Sphinx is Hor-m-akhet, or 'Horus who is on the horizon'. Horus was one of the chief Egyptian deities – a solar god – and his presence so near the royal tomb served to remind the king of the rising sun, a symbol of resurrection. Some 4,500 years old, 18 metres (60 feet) high and over 55 metres (180 feet) long, the Sphinx must repeatedly be cleared of the desert sands which threaten to bury it. Here, only its head and shoulders emerge above the surface.

Tourists, with the help of guides, clamber up the huge stone blocks that form an Egyptian pyramid, c. 1870 *(opposite)*. Produced with the forced labour of thousands of slaves, the pyramids remain marvels of engineering. According to William Flinders Petrie (1853–1942) who excavated many ancient Egyptian sites, errors in the angles and lengths of their construction could 'be covered with one's thumb'.

The ferryman who took the Scottish missionary and explorer David Livingstone across the Lulimala River in his dying days *(above left)*. Livingstone was on an expedition to find the source of the Nile, but succumbed to dysentery on 1 May 1873: his heart was buried in Africa, but his body was carried to Zanzibar and shipped back to Britain for burial.

Another associate of Livingstone's: the journalist and explorer Henry Stanley *(above right)*. Stanley (whose real name was John Rowlands) was sent to Africa by the *New York Herald* to find Livingstone, who was believed dead. Their famous meeting took place at Ujuji on Lake Tanganyika on 28 October 1871. As was the custom then, this photograph would have been used as Stanley's calling card.

A crowd enters Christiansberg Castle on the Gold Coast, now part of
Ghana, c. 1873 *(above)*. The names are witness to the country's colonial
past. The Portuguese, Dutch, Danish, Swedish, British and French all traded
off this coast, dealing in gold and slaves. Until the independence of Ghana
in 1957, the Gold Coast was a British colony.

More 'local colour' from the lens of Mrs Lekegian, this time featuring an
Egyptian mosque in the 1890s *(opposite)*. Not only was Egyptian culture
and civilization considerably more ancient than that of Europe, but the
country had also – with the Arab conquest of AD 641 – adopted Islam,
which lent it even greater exoticism for the nineteenth-century traveller.

A view from the entrance to a cave 2000 metres (7000 feet) up on Mount Elgon on the Uganda–Kenya border, taken by Ernest Gedge c. 1889. Frederick Jackson and a guide can be seen to the left of the scene. The climb took place during an expedition led by Jackson from Mombasa to Lake Victoria and Buganda, in an attempt to join up with Stanley who was moving from the Nile to the Indian Ocean.

An undated photograph *(above)* of a signalman and a baboon – one of
South Africa's indigenous animals – at Uitenhage near Port Elizabeth on
the southeastern coast of the Cape Province (formerly the British-ruled
Cape Colony). Railways were essential to the free movement of goods to
and from the interior, and during the latter half of the nineteenth century
various lines were built linking the diamond fields and later the gold fields
with outlets at the coast.

Chief Nguie, head of the village of Bolobo, situated on the western border
of Congo–Zaire, photographed by the Reverend G. Grenfell in the 1880s
*(opposite)*. After the decline of the mediaeval kingdom of Kongo which
centred around the banks of the Zaire River, the region fell into Belgian
hands and, around the time this picture was taken, became known as the
Congo Free State.

In a photograph dated c. 1901 *(opposite)*, a young woman from what would then have been Abyssinia (now Ethiopia) poses for the camera of L. Naretti and G. P. Devey. The subject's dress – or lack of it – and the curiously incongruous backdrop of balustrade and statuary all point to this being a studio picture taken by professional photographers for subsequent sale.

A portrait of the 'kaffir' chief Magato, in a portrait from around 1890 *(above left)*. Kaffir, from the Arabic *kafir*, or infidel, was a generic term used by white South Africans to describe the various Bantu-speaking African tribes of the Cape Province, notably the Xhosa. The term came to have racist overtones.

In a photograph taken by Captain H. G. C. Swayne in Somalia c. 1894, a man sits in front of the body of a black rhinoceros bull *(above right)*. This solitary, two-horned herbivore, *Diceros bicornis*, is 1.5 metres (5 feet) tall at the shoulder and provided a sizeable prey for hunters.

Canoes drift between the reeds at Kanyawanga on the eastern shore of
Lake Edward, in a photograph taken c. 1907 *(above)*. This was once an
important location on the salt trade route.

A group of Turkana dance around a tree in this 1906 photograph taken by
C. W. Hobbey *(opposite)*. For the Turkana, nomads living in an arid part of
northern Kenya, social activities such as dancing and other ceremonials are
only possible in the few months after a good rainy season. The rest of their
lives are spent on the move, finding fresh pastures for their herds, which are
essential to their survival.

A group of natives of Sierra Leone, West Africa, in about 1900 *(above)*.
Their headdresses are made from a framework of bones, elaborated with
human and animal skulls. The rattles on their legs serve to emphasize their
movements and so intensify the effect of any ritual of which they are part.

A 'jester' to Unyoro, a Ugandan king, photographed c. 1911 *(opposite)*. His
dress suggests that he may have had a magical role. African sorcerers and
healers cover themselves with the skins of wild beasts, and with animal
bones, teeth, and similar objects. The extraordinary and highly elaborate
costumes of this figure and of those above mark them out as having a
sacred function in their communities.

A man and a woman from Congo-Zaire show their tribal scarification and filed teeth. Creating decorative patterns of scars on the skin is a traditional custom in parts of Africa, and is done to beautify the face and body and as a sign of tribal identity, as is the filing of teeth. It can also be a mark of initiation or status. This photograph was taken in the 1900s by Sir Harry Johnston, a colonial administrator, anthropologist and geographer who studied native African peoples and their culture.

The heir to the throne – the boy destined to take on the role of Kabaka, king of the Baganda tribe who live west of Lake Victoria in Uganda, in another Johnston photograph from the 1900s. The serious expression on this boy's young face implies an awareness of his destiny. The Kabaka was a powerful figure around whom the workings of the kingdom of Buganda centred. In 1966, after Uganda became a republic, the then Kabaka – King Freddie – was forced into exile, and in 1967 Buganda, deprived of its status as a separate kingdom, was absorbed into the new republican state.

This photograph taken by Sir Harry Johnston in the 1900s shows a group of Kenyan fisherwomen. What appear to be outsized hats are, in fact, basketweave fish-traps, which can be upturned and worn on the head when not being used to catch fish.

In a photograph dated 1901, taken by L. Naretti and G. P. Devey, a group of young, native fishermen are seen with their rafts in the shallow waters near the port of Massawa (Mits'iwa) on the shores of the Red Sea in Eritrea, on Africa's northeast coast *(above)*. The sea is a valuable source of food in this drought-ridden region, shielded by the highlands of the interior from the rain-bearing winds that blow from the south.

A hunter with bow, quiver and knife stoops to drink from a pond in this photograph taken by Sir Harry Johnston in the 1900s *(opposite)*. According to the custom of his tribe, the man wears earrings which have stretched the lobes of his ears into sinewy strands of skin and flesh.

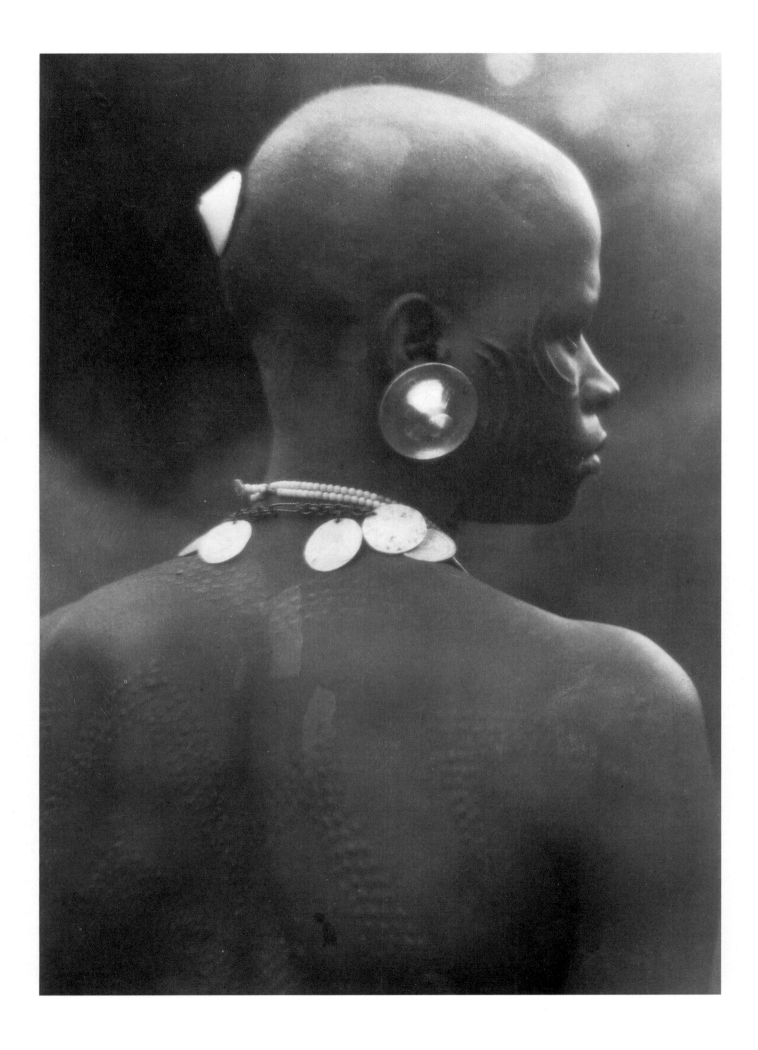

A Wacumba warrior from what is now Tanzania shows the traditional tribal pattern of scarring on his face and back, in a picture dating from around 1934 *(opposite)*. In order to create such scar patterns, the skin is lifted with a thorn and cut. Charcoal, grit or ash is then rubbed into the cut to allow the formation of scar tissue without infection.

Antlers, tusks, and skulls from opposite ends of Africa. The first photograph *(above left)*, taken by Major H. Schomburgh c. 1913, shows a man from Togo in West Africa wearing a horned headdress. The second picture *(above right)*, which dates from around 1906 and was taken by C. A. Reid, shows a cache of skulls and tusks in Mozambique, possibly a store for the ivory trade.

An elaborate weaving loom, photographed by L. Naretti and G. P. Devey in about 1901 in what is now Ethiopia. In certain African countries weaving is carried out by men, and this man may be one of the Dorze people of the Ethiopian highlands, who are famed for their weaving skills. The weaving of cloth from fibres may have originated in basketmaking.

Fisheries at Lake Kivu in a photograph taken c. 1912. The lake spans the
boundary between Congo–Zaire and Rwanda. Africans use a variety of
fishing tackle, from ordinary nets to the Kenyan fishing baskets seen on
page 122. Here, the fishermen are using hoops and nets to scoop up their
catch in the shallows. Large conical baskets hang from the elaborate
wooden framework above them.

A cane roof filters the glare of the hot sun and shades passers-by in a covered walkway in Fez, Morocco *(above)*. Reed is a traditional building material in Arab countries.

The ruins of Zimbabwe, which gave its name to the modern state formerly known as Southern Rhodesia, seen here in the 1920s *(opposite)*. Zimbabwe, which means 'stone house' in Bantu, was once the centre of a thriving Shona state. Using local granite, the Shona developed a system of building towering stone walls to screen their clay huts. The walls still stand as a reminder of the power of this once-great capital, which was at its peak between the thirteenth and sixteenth centuries.

Two photographs redolent of Africa's colonial past. The first *(opposite)* shows a black servant posing with a tray of champagne in his hands, in Tanganyika in about 1917. At the time this picture was taken, Tanganyika would have been passing from the hands of the Germans – who had colonised the country since 1884 – into those of the British, who wrested much of it from the Germans during World War I. Tanganyika finally threw off its colonial chains completely in 1964 when, together with Zanzibar, it formed the modern state of Tanzania under the presidency of Julius Nyere, known to his people as *Mwalimu* – the teacher.

In a posed picture dating from 1935-36, a labourer stands, pickaxe over his shoulder, in land being cleared for cultivation near Kasempa in northern Zambia *(above)*. Zambia was formerly the British protectorate of Northern Rhodesia named – like Southern Rhodesia – after the adventurer and politician Cecil Rhodes, whose ambition it was to establish a vast band of British territory stretching 'from Cape to Cairo'.

An old villager from Tashdirte, Morocco, in a photograph dating from around 1928 *(above)*. The man's physical features and dress show that his ethnic origins are different from those of the negroid peoples of Africa further south. Morocco was originally inhabited by the Berbers, a group of ancient peoples who once inhabited the entire Barbary Coast that stretched from Egypt to the Atlantic. By the eleventh century, however, after various invasions and the eventual spread of Arab rule across North Africa, the country came under the control of the Almoravids, a Muslim dynasty whose empire included Algeria and Spain as well as Morocco.

A group of women walk down a street in Algiers, c. 1923 *(opposite)*. Their puffy pantaloons and covered faces evoke the age of the Harem and the Arabian Nights. In terms of the development of Islam and its influence, however, the segregated Harem and the subordinate status of women was a relatively late development; the teachings of Mohammed gave women considerable freedom, and the Koran only requires modesty in dress.

A crowd of pygmies has been persuaded out of the jungle to be photographed, on a film location in Congo-Zaire. For these diminutive people, the Central African rainforest is more than just home: so intimate is their relationship with it that they refer to the forest as their 'mother'. Their small stature, on average 1.37 metres (4½ feet) tall, has long fascinated foreigners; the accumulation of fat on their buttocks – a physiological phenomenon known as *steatopygia* which acts as an emergency store of energy for the body – suggests that they may be of bushmanoid origin. The picture dates from about 1934.

Archetypal Africa – a lion attacks a zebra on the savanna. On closer inspection, however, the pair turn out to be fakes. They are stuffed animals, posed in a tableau that creates a popular image of Africa, rather like an exhibit in a museum. The photograph, which is undated, was taken in Kenya by Mrs Will Gordon.

An annual pilgrimage in Morocco in the 1920s. Pilgrimage – in particular, the *Hajj*, or pilgrimage to Mecca, the birthplace of Mohammed – is one of the five duties, or Pillars of the Faith, that devout Muslims are expected to perform. The others are bearing witness to the faith by reciting *Alahu Akbar*, 'God is Great'; performing *salat*, or prayer, five times a day; giving alms, or *zakat*; and fasting during Ramadhan, the ninth lunar month of the Muslim calendar. Careful observance of the duties on a daily basis makes the Muslim faith more than a religion – it is a way of life.

The sun sets over the harbour with its mosque at Moroni in the Comoros islands, in a photograph taken by Michael Freeman. Lying northwest of Madagascar, the Comoros are a melting pot of cultures. Originally occupied by peoples from as far apart as Africa, Asia and Indonesia, the islands were colonised by the French in 1912. In 1975 they gained their independence under the presidency of Ahmed Abdallah, and three years later were declared an Islamic federation.

In a photograph taken by Adrian Arbib, a young Kenyan boy has his head shaved by his mother *(opposite)*. The shaving of hair is part of the ritual that signifies the boy's coming to manhood.

Another Arbib photograph showing a young Masai *moran*, or warrior, blowing a kudu horn, which is a symbol of his age-set *(above)*. Masai society has an elaborate hierarchy based on age. When a boy reaches his mid-teens, he is initiated as a *moran* with all the other boys of his age-set. For up to fifteen years, these young men will live and work together until it is time for them to enter the next set, the *Ilterekeyani*, or junior elders. At subsequent intervals of fifteen years, they will be promoted to senior elders, retired elders, and, finally, to the oldest age-set of all. So reliable is this system that the Masai can trace their history from it, and historians have used it to date events as far back as the late eighteenth century.

A country village near the town of Bida, in the lush landscape near the
lower course of the river Niger in Nigeria, photographed by Sir Peter
Holmes *(above)*. With their round mud walls and thatched roofs, this cluster
of huts is typical of the building style found in many parts of Africa.

A salt miner from Taoudenni in northern Mali holds a slab of salt weighing
30 kilograms (66 pounds) *(opposite)*. Salt was once a highly prized
commodity in Africa. The photograph was taken by John Evans.

In a picture by Chris Caldicott, men on a steamer on the River Niger in Mali look down from the deck onto a boat loaded with wood. The wood may be a delivery of fuel for the steamer *(opposite)*.

A Tuareg camel train crosses the Algerian Sahara, in a photograph by Chris Bradley *(above left)*. The Tuareg are one of the Berber groups – a nomadic, aristocratic warrior class known as the 'Blue Men' after the blue veils worn by Tuareg males. In their traditional way of life, they roamed the Sahara – from southern Algeria to northern Nigeria, and from western Libya to Timbuktu, Mali – with their camel herds, trading salt from Algeria. The establishment of firmer national boundaries, however, has limited their former free-ranging lifestyle.

A Turkana woman, from northern Kenya, carries food on her head *(above right)*. The aridness of the region in which the Turkana live makes permanent settlement impossible, and the people live a pastoral life. Their animals are their chief source of food. The traditional Turkana diet consists of milk, most often drunk sour or turned into ghee (clarified butter), meat, and occasionally blood taken from their animals and mixed into soups or sour milk. The photograph was taken by Adrian Arbib.

Sahara sands meet the River Niger as it flows through Mali in this photograph by Chris Caldicott. Rising in the highlands of Guinea, the river curves northeast through Mali before turning southward again into Nigeria, eventually to disgorge into the Atlantic. Its total course is 4185 kilometres (2600 miles), making it the third-longest river in Africa. The first European to see the river was the Scotsman Mungo Park, on his expedition of 1796. On a second expedition in 1805, Park started the descent of the Niger near Timbuktu but died near the Bussa Rapids, a short distance down the river.

Flamingos flock in their thousands to the Ngorongoro Crater in Tanzania. These tall wading birds, which are part of the stork family and can reach 1.25 metres (4 feet) in height, gather together in large numbers in shallow waters and mud, where they sift for food with their beaks. Flamingos are just one of the many forms of wildlife that crowd the Ngorongoro: large herds of wildebeest, zebra and gazelle may also be seen here. The photograph was taken by Michael Freeman.

In a village near Betafo in the central uplands of Madagascar, two farmers set off for work walking along Route 34, which leads to Miandrivazo *(opposite)*. The style of the two buildings behind them is characteristic of the region. Houses of this type are built by the Merina people who are of Indonesian origin. As in the Chinese practice of feng shui, the orientation of each house and the siting of the functions within it is crucial: the building itself must face west, the kitchen must be in the south, and the bed of the master of the household must be in the northeast corner, the holy place of the ancestors. The photograph was taken by John R. Jones.

A Dinka man from southern Sudan, photographed by John Miles *(above left)*. The Dinka live around the network of rivers that flow into the White Nile. They number about one million, and are primarily cattle herders.

In this photograph by John Evans *(above right)*, a young woman from Mali has been spattered with cement paste used in the plastering of a thatched dwelling. In the past, mud, the ubiquitous substance used for all kinds of building work in Africa, would probably have been used instead.

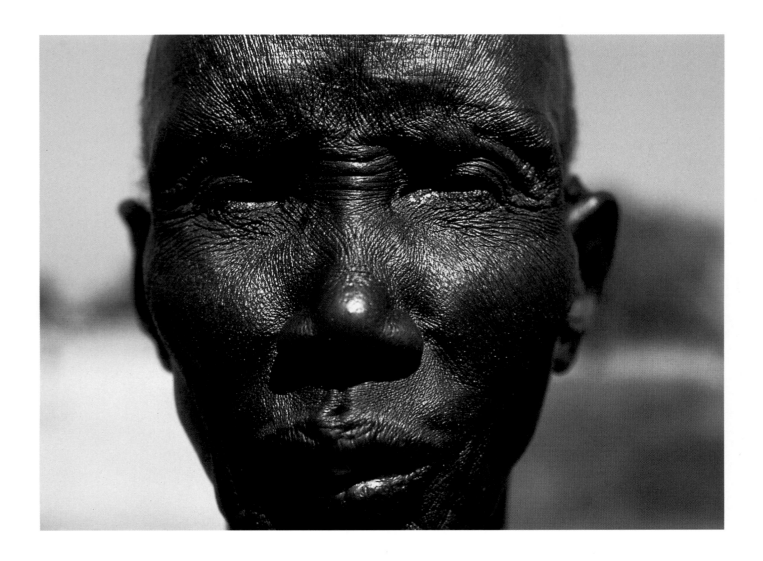

Two generations of Dinka from Bahr el Ghazal province in southern
Sudan *(above* and *opposite)*, photographed by John Miles. Although many
years separate the man and the boy, both display the characteristic Dinka
features of long, narrow face, small chin and high cheekbones. The Dinka
are nomads who follow their herds from one pasture to another. Unlike
the closely knit and highly structured societies of more settled peoples, the
Dinka live in isolation from each other and their culture is egalitarian, with
no kings or rulers.

On a stretch of sand blown into ridges and furrows by the desert wind, a woman sits facing the oasis of Siwa, in the Sahara near Egypt's northwest border with Libya. The photograph was taken by Chris Caldicott.

Every February, a sacred mile along the River Sokoto near Argungu in northwest Nigeria is traditionally the setting for a frenzy of fishing, as this picture by Sir Peter Holmes shows. The occasion is the Argungu Fishing Festival, in which thousands of competitors from all over Nigeria have just forty-five minutes to see who can land the best catch. In their nets, the fishermen can trap Nile perch weighing up to 64 kilograms (140 pounds); they may keep the smaller ones, but they present the larger fish to the emirs who run the festival.

A priest and a deacon from from the churches of Lalibella in northern Ethiopia *(opposite* and *above).* The churches have been carved out of the solid rock, and were built in this way after King Lalibella had a dream instructing him to build a New Jerusalem. The king's way of honouring the dream was to construct twelve churches – one for each apostle – hewn out of the rock itself. The photographs were taken in 1996 by Norma and Maurice Joseph respectively.

Fishing between the villages of Analalava and Ambanje, near Maromandia in northwest Madagascar. The coastline here is indented with inlets of the Mozambique Channel, which separates the island from the mainland of Africa. The warm tropical sea and lagoons ensure a plentiful supply of fish. The photograph was taken by John R. Jones.

the Poles

# to the ends of the earth

## Sir Ranulph T-W-Fiennes Bt. O.B.E.

BACK IN 1972 MY WIFE SUGGESTED we should travel around the Earth's surface on its circumpolar axis. Ten years later we did so and began a love-hate relationship with the polar regions which still holds us spellbound. The Norwegians call it *polarhulle*, a yearning forever to return to the far, dark, cold places.

Humans have hunted along the edge of the Arctic Ocean for thousands of years. Vast tracts of Siberian and Canadian territory are within the Arctic Circle and the long history of merchant navigators, viking sailors, fortune seekers and audacious sealing captains is well documented.

Human involvement in the far south is another matter altogether. As late as the nineteenth century, tough whalers working the icy waters were wont to say: 'Beyond 40 degrees south is no law. Beyond 50 degrees south no God.' Bearing in mind that the city of London lies at 52 degrees north, it seems extraordinary that mankind should have taken so long to cross the Southern Polar circle (Cook did so only in 1770) and for the first explorers to travel any distance towards the centre of mainland Antarctica only in 1904.

### PERILOUS SEAS

The reason for the relatively short history of South Polar exploration is the great barrier of the Southern Ocean, as hostile to man as the ice continent it surrounds. *The Antarctic Pilot* states: 'Navigation in this area is rendered difficult by sea-ice, violent weather changes, dangerous shoals, large seas and swells, instability of compass, inadequate charts, absence of navigation aids and whiteout.'

Frank Worsley, captain of Shackleton's ship *Endurance* described it thus: 'The great unceasing swell of the Southern Ocean rolls almost unchecked around this end of the world in the roaring forties and the stormy fifties. The highest, broadest swells in the world, rising to forty or fifty feet and more from hollow to crest, rage in disorder during gales. At times their crests sweep up until their front forms an almost perpendicular wall of green, rushing water that smashes on a ship's deck, flattening steel bulwarks and crushing deckhouses like eggshells. These blue water hills in a heavy gale move as fast as twenty-five miles an hour. The impact of hundreds of tons of solid water at this speed is difficult to imagine.'

Nevertheless, once the Arctic Circle had been ruthlessly 'fished out', it was the sea harvest of the nutrient-rich Southern Ocean that lured whalers and sealers to the very edge of ice-girt Antarctica. In 1938, despite previous regulatory agreements signed internationally, 50,000 whales were slaughtered for their oil. Many species of Southern whale were driven to the edge of extinction. Against 250,000 great blue whales known to exist in 1900, the South Georgia whaling fleets of 1965 counted only four blues all year.

Seal populations fared little better. Over five million fur seals have been clubbed to death in Antarctica. As long ago as 1829, an observer described the decline in their numbers: 'This harvest of the seas has been so effectively reaped that not a single seal has been seen although it is only a few years since countless multitudes covered these same beaches.' Although many species of whale and seal are gradually increasing their

In a photograph taken c. 1879 by E. M. Langworthy, a boat sails past floating pack ice in the waters around Norway. In the Arctic, ice masses that have broken adrift from the polar cap are carried towards the Atlantic by a south-flowing current.

numbers again, there is now a new danger: the effects of pollution, of oil spillage and global warming may yet prove even more lethal than the nineteenth-century hunters.

## HUMAN IMPACT

The only people who can be said to inhabit the great frozen continent – a bigger land mass than North America – are the isolated scientists, most of whom work at their coastal bases only during the short summer season. A mere handful stay through the long dark winter, and only a tiny percentage see Antarctica beyond the confines of their centrally heated huts. The science bases (forty-two in 1971) used their local crevasses or cliffsides as garbage tips until, in the 1980s, Greenpeace embarrassed them into cleaning up their image along with, in the case of a single U.S. base, over 2000 tonnes of waste including oil drums, chemicals and explosives.

At present the threat to Antarctica from manmade pollution is probably small. Geologists are not likely to locate minerals at commercially viable levels and existing treaties discourage prospecting. Oil tankers should not run aground as they have in the Arctic, although increasing numbers of cruise ships call every summer. Some 6000 tourists are briefly disgorged to ogle deserted science bases, penguin colonies and spectacular scenery. Mostly they behave well enough and are warned not to interfere with the fauna. One disaster did occur, however, when an Argentinian ship, the *Bahia Paradzso*, ran aground in 1989, spilling 900,000 litres of oil and devastating the locality, the fish and the birds that eat them.

## DRIVING FORCES

If tourists and the majority of scientists have little or no contact with Antarctica's great interior, who does? Who are the Antarctic's explorers of our times and what are their motives?

In the main they are individuals, often from Norway and Britain, and their stated reasons for risking life and limb are legion. Wally Herbert, one of Europe's greatest living polar explorers, said: 'And of what value was this journey? It is as well for those who ask such a question that there are others who feel the answer and never need to ask.'

Amundsen described the lure of territory where no human had previously set foot, while Shackleton spoke of a call to adventure and glory: 'Why seek the Pole? War in the old days made men. We have not the same stirring time to live in and must look for other outlets for our energy and for the restless spirit that fame alone can satisfy.'

In similar vein, speaking of Vivian Fuchs, Edmund Hillary said, 'I felt his underlying urge came more from an honest love of adventure and the pride and prestige that he felt would accrue to his country and himself if he were first to succeed in such a long and hazardous venture.'

But Elspeth Huxley probably came nearest to the mark when she wrote: 'What persuaded these men to seek out hardships so extreme that most ordinary mortals would give all they possess to avoid them? . . . Fame and fortune . . . also love of country, lust for adventure, devotion for a cause, and more obscure forces like an urge towards martyrdom. Certainly there is a curiosity, a desire to know what lies over the next hill, on the

Longyearbyen on Advent Bay, Spitsbergen, in a photograph taken by J. M. Wordie in 1919. Spitsbergen is the main island in the Norwegian archipelago known as Svalbard.

moon and beyond the stars. All such motives are mixed together and the analyst who tries to sort them out and label them is generally wasting his time.'

## HAZARDS AND HARDSHIPS

At the time of writing, nobody has crossed Antarctica without outside support. Those who try find that the risks, the dangers and the discomforts have remained largely unchanged since the days of Amundsen and Scott. To cross 3000 kilometres of ice, much of it at high altitudes, without resupply means carrying some 230 kilograms per person. Shackleton dreamed of such a journey but the *Endurance* sank before he could begin it. His main worries were cold, hunger and crevasses.

As the year 2000 approaches, Shackleton's successors will find modern research and development has done little to provide answers to these basic problems. Food still weighs the same as it did despite the advent of dehydrated goodies because, in a waterless continent of ice, extra fuel is needed for rehydration. Clothing and footwear have advanced in many areas but not for manhaul sledgers needing to drag ultra-heavy weights which cause sweating that leads to hyperthermia unless the clothing is 100 percent breathable. Only tight-weave cotton is suitable and it was on the market in 1901. Radios were available to Amundsen and Scott and, then as now, they are at their least dependable in polar zones due to solar flares, polar cap absorption and other ionespheric disturbances.

Today's sledge runners experience the same problems as did Scott's. When fresh snowflakes fall they retain a beautiful hexagonal shape but the snow crystals of the Antarctic plateaux have been damaged by repeated collisions with other crystals as they are blown about in storms. Often enough the resulting surface, especially in low temperatures, grasps sledge runners as would the sand of a beach dune, maximizing friction.

Crevasses still lurk and no machine is available to tell the modern traveller where not to tread. When the Australian Antarctic explorer Douglas Mawson used dogs to haul his sledges, he had as much trouble with crevasses as any manhauler, losing animals in treacherous openings in the ice. Travelling day after day, month after month over such invisible traps saps away at an Antarctic traveller's confidence and morale.

The winds, too, are a constant source of worry for they bring whiteout and blizzard, frostbite and disorientation. Katabatic (gravity fed) winds roar from higher plateaux from zero to over a hundred knots with little or no warning. Tents can be torn away from sleeping sledgers. In 1903, Scott's men sheltered on the *Discovery* from one such blizzard. He wrote: 'If a man ventured as far as the deck he gasped for breath and half-suffocated with ears, eyes and nose stuffed with snow. A bitch with a litter of puppies was found with her tongue torn out, frozen to the feeding tin.' Mawson recorded winds in excess of 300 kilometres an hour.

Even the sun can be an enemy when coupled with the endless snowfields and the cold. Goggles will mist up and, when their owner removes them in order to see, he can quickly suffer snowblindness. In a whiteout the snow floor reflects and refracts the glare so that there is zero perception of depth to human

Another photograph by Wordie also dating from 1919, showing what was then known as Adolf Bay and Pyramid Mountain as seen from Point Napier on Spitsbergen.

vision and lurking crevasses are not detected. Huxley once decribed how Scott '. . . was in agony from sunblindness which even cocaine could not alleviate. The victim of this horrible complaint felt as though his eyeballs were being tattooed by red-hot needles or brushed with gritty sand.'

Manhaulers, then and now, suffer from piles and crutch-rot so that every step rubs raw skin on raw skin. Frostbite of fingers, toes, ears and nose leaves blisters and often gangrene. Splitting headaches, breathing difficulties and nausea from the altitude do not help.

Mawson, on an early expedition described by his biographer, '. . . lowered his thick underpants and a shower of skin fragments and hair fell into the snow. Strips of skin had vanished from his legs. His kneecaps were without cover, just roughly rippled flesh, his private parts were red and raw from the friction of walking. His soles had separated into insoles of dead skin which came away leaving abraded raw tissue. An abundant watery fluid filled his socks. He replaced his own separated soles and bound them back in place with bandages.'

All the great journeys of Antarctic history tell of tension and friction between participants exacerbated through such physical hardships. Of Scott's 1911 expedition, Apsley Cherry Garrard wrote '. . . the loss of a biscuit crumb left a sense of injury which lasted for a week . . . . The greatest of friends were so much on another's nerves that they did not speak for days for fear of quarrelling . . . . Scott and Shackleton were wholly incompatible, the strains of the journey made feelings boil over and any triviality was enough to detonate an explosion.'

## VASTNESS OF ICE

Before Shackleton and subsequent explorers could even reach the mainland of the continent they had hundreds of miles of floating ice-shelf to traverse. The Ross Ice Shelf, hinged to the mainland, is bigger than Texas but could theoretically break off in its entirety at any time. Every year huge icebergs do split from the Ross and other such ice shelves, but ice from the high plateaux constantly replaces the losses as it pours eternally down via gigantic glaciers that have to be seen to be believed.

One such is the Beardmore Glacier which I once tried inadequately to describe in my diary: 'The horizons which now opened up to us in slow motion were awesome, a sprawling mass of rock and ice in suspended motion. This was the headwater of a moving ice-river. Constrictions caused by the 15,000-feet-high mountains had formed, and were even now renewing savage whirlpools and maelstroms of cascading pressure-ice. Huge open chasms leered from distant foothills and standing ice-waves reared up at the base of black truncated cliffs. I found this canvas full of power and wonder and thanked God for this moment of being alive. Nothing else lived here nor ever had since the dinosaurs of Gondwanaland. No birds nor beasts nor the least bacteria survived. Only the deep roar of massive avalanche, the shriek and grind of splitting rock, the groan of shifting ice and the music, soft or fierce, of the winds from a thousand valleys, moved to and fro across the eternal silence.'

Further down the course of its 300-metre descent the Beardmore, the second largest glacier in the world, stretches to fifty kilometres in width and pours down its valley in a cataract

The desolate landscape of Greenland as portrayed by B. B. Roberts c. 1933. The interior is blanketed by a vast glacier 3400 metres (11000 feet) deep in parts.

of spectacular chaos, a devil's cauldron with crevasses large enough to devour St Paul's Cathedral. In 1990 the great Tyrolean climber Reinhold Messner, an expert at crossing unstable ice, was lost here. 'We found no way out,' he wrote. 'Like blind men we had run into the middle of the abysses and holes, into a labyrinth of ice towers and crevasses more than 200 feet deep.'

On smoother snakes of escalator moraine ice, rocks rich in minerals split from the Beardmore's valley walls to ride majestically down the glacier to the ice shelf and eventually out to sea on icebergs. Sometimes all of a berg's ice above the sea's surface will melt so that sailors gaze only at the miraculous sight of a giant boulder apparently afloat on the Southern Ocean.

The Antarctic ice sheet is, in fact, a single vast glacier bigger than the USA and containing seventy-five percent of the world's fresh water. Scientists currently argue as to whether the undoubted global warming will cause more ice to form or a lethal meltdown submerging all the world's coastal cities, one of many 'catastrophe scenarios' which the followers of scientific hypothesis have produced. However, it is worth remembering that, only 10,000 years ago, the Laurentide, a glacier even bigger than Antarctica, covered both Canada and North America. Yet now it is gone, a mere scientific memory.

There is also concern about the hole in the ozone layer, discovered in 1985 by British scientists, which lies twenty-four kilometres above Antarctica and allows dangerous levels of UV light to descend unfiltered to Antarctica and southern lands like Australia and Patagonia. Every year the hole grows bigger and more animals including humans suffer the resulting cancers, blindness and weakened immune systems. International concern has mounted and Antarctica is proving to be the best place for monitoring the health of our planet.

## THE FAMILIAR NORTH

In terms of wonder and curiosity, the Arctic is altogether less appealing than its southern counterpart. After all the North Pole and the Arctic Ocean surrounding it are at sea level and offer no great glaciers nor mountain ranges, no tragic deaths of polar heroes nor threats of spectacular meltdown. Altogether more accessible to ice-strengthened tourist ships and flown over daily by most European and North American airlines, the Arctic is far more familiar to most of us.

People live there all their lives – the Inuit of Canada, Alaska and Siberia, the Lapps of Scandinavia. Oil and minerals are drilled and mined there and polar bears have suffered so much television coverage that their mystique has long since dissipated. Greenland, Spitsbergen and the lands of the Canadian Archipelago, the home of the musk ox and the lemming, are all rich in scenic splendour and each region has its fascinating tales of early exploration. But somehow none has stirred the international imagination in the same way as the 'romantic age of exploration' in Antarctica.

Two survivors from the wreck of a Norwegian sealer are seen here on Spitsbergen, having joined the Arctic expedition led by Sir Martin Conway (*opposite*). The photograph dates from 1896.

Members of Captain Robert Falcon Scott's first Antarctic expedition look on as a balloon is deflated. During this ambitious and heavily equipped British expedition, which began in 1901, Scott used anchored balloons as route markers. On this occasion, he and his team penetrated as far as 82° 17' South, about 800 kilometres (500 miles) from the South Pole's 90° South. The photograph was taken in 1904, the final year of the expedition.

Stranded on Elephant Island, Shackleton's men cheer the approach of the
relief boat, photographed by Frank Hurley. Ernest Shackleton had been
with Scott on his 1901–04 Antarctic expedition, and in 1907–09
commanded his own expedition. In 1914 he set off for Antarctica again but
in October of the following year his ship, the *Endurance*, was crushed in
pack ice. Knowing that he and his men faced certain death unless help
could be found, Shackleton set off in an open boat to cross the 1300
kilometres (800 miles) of sea to South Georgia. He arrived there on 20
May 1916, and on 25 August returned to collect his men with four boats
and a Chilean tug, completing one of the most famous rescues in history.

Two photographs taken by Frank Hurley on Shackleton's 1914–16 Antarctic expedition. Using a delaying device on one camera, Hurley captures himself with a second camera on the ice *(opposite)*. The expedition party enjoys a midwinter dinner *(above right)*.

Scott and his party stare defeat in the face *(above left)*. On reaching the South Pole on 18 January 1912, they find a tent left by the Norwegian explorer Roald Amundsen who had beaten them to their goal by thirty-five days, having arrived at the Pole on 14 December 1911. Inside the tent – which he had christened *Polheim*, or 'pole home' – Amundsen had left letters for Scott and for the king of Norway, in case he should not make it back to his ship, the *Fram*, waiting at Framheim near the Bay of Whales. In fact, he and his party made the return journey in only forty-one days.

Scott and his men in a photograph taken by Herbert Ponting in April 1911, just three months into his fatal expedition to the South Pole *(above)*. A series of misjudgments contributed to Scott's failure. His insistence on using snow tractors, which broke down, and ponies, which died in the polar conditions, as well as his strategy of sending back to base any team that was weak or no longer useful, meant that by January 1912 only one small group of just five men – Scott himself, Dr. Wilson, lieutenants H. R. Bowers and L.E.G Oates, and Edgar Evans – made it to the Pole. None survived the return journey: Evans died in the tent, Oates famously walked out to his death, and Scott, Wilson and Bowers were found dead in their sleeping bags, within a mere 18 kilometres (11 miles) of a food depot.

Food to sustain Antarctic explorers: Herbert Ponting creates a memorable image, an advertisement for Heinz Baked Beans. The photograph was taken in June 1911*(opposite)*.

The 'ramparts' of a castle-like iceberg loom above the small rider with his sledge and dog team, in this picture by Herbert Ponting dating from September 1911. These floating ice mountains fascinated the first polar travellers. Martin Frobisher, an Elizabethan pirate, navigator and explorer, was the first to suggest that icebergs were not separate ice masses that had formed in the freezing seas, but in fact enormous chunks of ice that had broken away from even larger glaciers.

The night watch: some of Ernest Shackleton's crew warm themselves by a blaze on the *Endurance* during the 1914–1916 expedition to Antarctica, in this photograph by Frank Hurley (*above*). The expedition's goal – which was never realised – was to cross Antarctica from the Weddell Sea to the Ross Sea.

A grotto in an Antarctic iceberg, with a glimpse of the *Terra Nova* in the distance, as photographed by Herbert Ponting (*opposite*). This was the whaling ship on which the ill-fated Scott and his team, which included meteorologists and geophysicists, embarked for Antarctica in 1910 in what became a race to beat Amundsen to the South Pole. In January 1911, the *Terra Nova* anchored at McMurdo Sound, thus making Scott's journey to the Pole 160 kilometres (100 miles) longer than that facing Amundsen, who had anchored near the Bay of Whales.

Two photographs taken by Frank Hurley during Shackleton's 1914-16 expedition to the Antarctic. The first *(opposite)* shows Dr. Hussey with 'Samson' and an unnamed dog; the second *(above right)* shows Wild with two dogs on the *Endurance*.

Captain Oates with some of the Siberian ponies used as sledge animals instead of dogs on Scott's last expedition of 1910-12, photographed by Herbert Ponting *(above left)*. Although ponies could pull heavy loads and ate less than dogs in relation to their body weight, they could not withstand Antarctic conditions as well. They could not curl up like dogs to keep warm in a blizzard, nor could they be fed on the meat of their dead fellows, as was the custom with dogs. The use of ponies contributed to the failure of this expedition, in which Oates sacrificed his life, knowingly walking out to his death in the blizzard with the now-famous words: 'I am just going outside and may be some time.'

The *Endurance* enters pack ice in the northeast corner of the Weddell Sea, during the early part of Shackleton's 1914–16 expedition to cross Antarctica via the South Pole. The ice had formed early and was unusually thick for the time of year: Shackleton likened the patterns it formed to some gigantic jigsaw invented by nature. Several days were lost waiting for conditions to improve but, by January 1915, it was too late: the *Endurance* was trapped and worse was to come.

The progressive destruction of the *Endurance* by pack ice, 480 kilometres (300 miles) from land, in two photographs taken by Frank Hurley *(above* and *opposite)*. Unable to free the ship from the floating ice in which it was caught, the crew drifted with it for several months. In August 1915 they abandoned ship and made camp on the ice. In October, the *Endurance* was finally crushed, and in November what remained of it sank. All that the crew were able to salvage were three open boats, some equipment and some supplies.

A photograph of an Inuit couple by Dr L. Koch c. 1920 *(above left)*, and a close-up of an Inuit child taken by Colonel Andrew Croft in about 1934 during the British Trans-Greenland Expedition *(above right)*. The Inuit are believed to be the descendants of peoples who migrated to the North American continent across the Bering Strait thousands of years ago. Their traditional way of life was perfectly adapted to an existence in the harsh, polar regions. Many polar explorers – Amundsen among them – learned their survival techniques from the Inuit.

The ice-covered wastes of Queen Maud Mountains in the west of Antarctica near the Ross Ice Shelf, relatively close to the South Pole *(opposite)*. The photograph was taken in November 1960 during the Nimrod Expedition. The goal of such modern expeditions is scientific study, but the name of this particular expedition recalls an earlier spirit of discovery – the *Nimrod* was the ship on which Shackleton set off in 1907 on a journey that would bring him 88° 23' South, less than two degrees off the South Pole's 90°.

In a photograph by Charles Swithinbank dated 13 March 1960, the icebreaker USS *Atka* looms above the icebound waters off McMurdo Station, an American base on Antarctica's Ross Ice Shelf. The outline of volcanic Mount Erebus, rising 3794 metres (12,450 feet) above sea level, can be glimpsed in the background. The ghosts of old explorers are seen in the names: McMurdo was the first mate of the *Terror*, companion to the *Erebus*, commanded by James Clark Ross on his 1841 Antarctic expedition.

A view of Ellsworth Mountains in Antarctica, lying at 80° South, photographed by Bruce Herrod. The mountains flank the Ronne Ice Shelf, and their highest peak is the Vinson Massif, rising to 4897 metres (16,066 feet). The coastline here forms a ragged silhouette of inlets comprising ice streams, promontories and 'ice rises'.

A camp belonging to a joint US-UK geological survey party in the Thiel Mountains, Antarctica, photographed by Charles Swithinbank in December 1983. Where once polar exploration had been a matter of personal and national rivalry, the signing of the Antarctic Treaty of 1959 established Antarctica as a protected region of special scientific interest. Since then, in a spirit of international cooperation, many different nations have set up research stations there.

Letting off a flare in Antarctica, in a picture taken by Sir Ranulph Fiennes during his Transglobe Expedition of 1979-82 *(above)*. This was the first surface journey to be made around the world's polar axis. By the time he undertook this expedition, Fiennes was already a seasoned explorer, having negotiated the White Nile in 1969, the Jostedalsbre Glacier, Norway in 1970, and Headless Valley, Canada in 1971.

Brian Davison makes the first ascent of Mount Carse in South Georgia, in this photograph by Stephen Venables *(opposite)*. South Georgia lies in the sub-Antarctic region of the South Atlantic, at approximately the same latitude as the southernmost tip of Tierra del Fuego.

In a photograph by Martha Holmes, chinstrap penguins move over the Antarctic ice against a flotilla of icebergs *(opposite)*. Ungainly on land, penguins move fluidly and easily in the water. A large proportion of their bodies is made up of fat which can, by means of a highly efficient body mechanism, be transformed into heat, and it is this that enables them to withstand the freezing temperatures of their polar home. The fat is accumulated during periods of intense feeding, when fat stores can account for as much as twenty-five percent of a penguin's body weight – more even than that of whales or seals.

Midnight at 66° 1' North: looking down past an expedition meeting point towards one of the fjords near Angmagssalik, just south of the Arctic Circle on Greenland's east coast *(above)*. Much of Greenland's coastline is indented by such steep-sided inlets. The photograph was taken by Drew Geldart.

A photograph by Martha Holmes, showing a barnacled whale breaking the waves *(above)*. At the beginning of the twentieth century, hundreds of thousands of whales swam the world's oceans. Whaling, however, has brought them close to extinction. Because of their low reproduction rate, those that have survived and are now protected will be slow to replenish their numbers.

A bird's-eye view of the *Southern Quest* surrounded by pancake ice in Antarctica, in a photograph by Roger Mear *(opposite)*. Technological developments mean that polar travel is no longer the highly dangerous adventure it was for the first intrepid explorers. Electronic equipment on vessels such as these allows crews to keep in touch with the outside world. Modern explorers also have the option of reconnaissance by air; in Antarctica, in particular, aeroplanes and satellites have proved the most successful vehicles for studying the continent's inhospitable wastes.

the Middle East

# desert and oasis

Sir Wilfred Thesiger

I JOINED AL AUF, WHO WAS HERDING the camels, and we sat together in the twilight and talked of the journey ahead. He had crossed the eastern Sands two years before. He told me he was worried about the condition of some of the Bait Kathir camels. He doubted if they would be able to cross the Uruq al Shaiba, which he described as mountains of sand. I asked if we could avoid them, but he said they extended a week's journey to the west and ended in the east against the Umm al Samim, those legendary quicksands of which Bertram Thomas had heard the Bedu speak. Cross the Uruq al Shaiba we must, he said, if we were to reach Dhafara and the oasis of Liwa. I had heard the Bait Kathir use the expression 'as far as Dhafara' to describe the limit of the world . . . .

Four days after leaving Mughshin we reached Khaur bin Atarit, discovered by some forgotten Bedu but still bearing his name. The well was drifted in, but we dug it out. The water, as I expected, was very brackish and would get worse the longer it remained in the goatskins. Musallim made porridge for our evening meal, the only meal of the day. From now on we should be eating gritty lumps of unleavened bread smeared with a little butter. Bin Kabina poured water over our outstretched hands. This was the last time we should wash, even our hands, until we reached the wells at Dhafara.

In the morning we gave the camels another drink. Several refused to touch the bitter-tasting water, so we held up their heads and poured it down their throats. We filled the skins and plugged the tiny dribbling holes. The others said their midday prayers; then we loaded the camels and led them away between the golden dunes. We went on foot, for the full skins were heavy on their backs. The next morning we found a little parched herbage on the flank of a high dune and let our camels graze for two hours. Where we camped the dunes were very big, whale-back massifs rising above white plains of powdery gypsum. The scene was bleak and cheerless, curiously arctic in appearance. Twice I woke in the night and each time Sultan was brooding over the fire. We started again at sunrise and four hours later came to large red dunes, close together, covered with green plants, the result of heavy rain two years before. Fresh camel tracks showed that the Bait Musan were camped nearby: Sultan and the Bait Kathir went off to find them. Bin Kabina warned me that the Bait Kathir were going to make trouble.

## NO TURNING BACK

When they came back Sultan informed me that, as our camels were in poor condition and the Bait Musan said there was no grazing ahead, it would be madness to go on. Anyway we were short of food and water. The Bait Kathir were prepared to travel with me in the Sands to the east before rejoining the others near the coast. They would on no account try to cross the Empty Quarter. I asked al Auf if he would come with me and he said quietly, 'We have come here to go to Dhafara. If you want to go on I will guide you.' I asked bin Kabina and he answered that where I went he would go. I knew Musallim was jealous of Sultan. When I asked him he said, 'I will come,' whereupon his kinsman Mabkhaut volunteered to join us. The others said nothing. Once again we divided up the food. We took our share,

Stopping for a coffee break on the northeastern edge of the Nafud desert in 1911. The Nafud is now part of Saudi Arabia, and the photograph was taken by Captain W. I. Shakespear, who witnessed the coming of the new kingdom.

fifty pounds of flour, some of the butter and coffee, what remained of the sugar and tea, and a few dried onions. We also took four skins of water, choosing those that did not leak. Later, after much haggling and for an exorbitant price, we bought a spare camel from the Bait Musan . . . .

Next morning the Bait Kathir helped us load our camels; we said goodbye, picked up our rifles and set off. The Rashid took the lead, their faded brown clothes harmonising with the sand: al Auf a lean, neat figure, very upright; bin Kabina more loosely built, striding beside him. The two Bait Kathir followed close behind with the spare camel tied to Musallim's saddle. Their clothes, which had once been white, had become neutral-coloured from long use. Mabkhaut was the same build as al Auf, whom he resembled in many ways, though he was a less forceful character. Musallim, compactly built, slightly bow-legged and physically tough, was of a different breed. The least attractive of my companions, his character had suffered from too frequent sojourns in Muscat and Salala.

## THE BEDU WAY

The sands here were covered with yellow-flowering tribulus, heliotrope and a species of sedge. In the Sands, even in areas that have been barren for years, vegetation will spring up after rain and if the rain has been really heavy it may remain green, with even a further shower, for as long as four years. After two hours we encountered a small boy, dressed in the remnants of a loincloth, herding camels. He was from the Rashid and led us to a camp nearby. Here three men sat round the embers of a fire.

They had no tent; their only possessions were saddles, ropes, bowls and empty goatskins, and their weapons. Bedu such as these, having located grazing, which is often very hard to find, move on to it in the autumn. They remain there, sometimes a hundred miles from the nearest well, for six or seven months until the weather becomes hot . . . .

These men were very cheerful and full of life. The grazing was good; their camels, several in milk, would soon be fat. Life by their standards would be easy this year, but tonight they would sleep naked on the freezing sand, covered only with their flimsy loincloths. There were other years, such as al Auf had that very morning described to me, when the exhausted men rode back to the wells, to speak through blackened, bleeding lips of desolation in the Sands, of emptiness such as I had seen on the way here from Mughshin; when the last withered plants were gone and walking skeletons of men and beasts sank down to die. I thought of the bitter wells in the furnace heat of summer when hour by reeling hour men watered thirsty, thrusting camels, till at last the wells ran dry and importunate camels moaned for water that was not there. I thought how desperately hard were the lives of the Bedu in this weary land, how gallant and enduring was their spirit. The milk they gave us at sunset was soothing, in contrast to the bitter water which had rasped our throats. In the morning they handed us a small goatskin full of milk to take with us . . . .

Our hosts bade us go in peace and we wished them the safe-keeping of God. There were no more Arabs ahead of us until we reached Dhafara. At first the dunes were separate

The Haiyaniya fort and wells on the eastern edge of the Nafud desert, in a photograph by Captain Shakespear dating from 1911. The importance of Shakespear's pictures, taken in the Arabian Peninsula in the early years of the century, lies in the fact that they are the only photographic record of the rise of the House of Saud and the foundation of Saudi Arabia.

mountains of brick-red sand, rising above ash-white gypsum flats ringed with the vivid green of salt-bushes. Later they were even higher – 500 feet or more – and honey-coloured. At sunset al Auf doled out to each of us a pint of water mixed with milk, our ration for the day. After we had eaten the bread that Musallim cooked, bin Kabina took the small brass coffee-pot from the fire and served us with a few drops each. We piled more wood upon the fire, long snake-like roots of tribulus, warmed ourselves for a while and then lay down to sleep. A chill wind blew in gusts, charged with a spray of sand. I was happy in the company of these men who had chosen to come with me; I felt affection for them personally, and sympathy with their way of life. But though the easy quality of our relationship satisfied me, I did not delude myself that I could be one of them. Nevertheless I was their companion, and an inviolable bond united us, as sacred as the bond between host and guest, transcending loyalties of tribe and family. Because I was their companion on the road they would fight even against their own tribesmen in my defence, and would expect me to do the same. But I knew that for me the hardest test would be to live with them in harmony and not to let impatience master me; neither to withdraw into myself, nor to become critical of standards and ways of life different from my own.

Next morning we found a small patch of grazing and for an hour or two let our camels graze. Before going on we collected bundles of tribulus to feed to them in the evening. We were worried about our water: all the skins were sweating and there had been a regular ominous drip from them throughout the day. There was nothing we could do but press on, yet to push the camels too hard would founder them. They were already showing signs of thirst. After we had fed, al Auf decided we must go on again. We rode for hours along a salt flat. The dunes on either side, colourless in the moonlight, seemed higher by night than by day. Eventually we halted, and numbly we dismounted. I would have given much for a hot drink, but I knew I must wait eighteen hours for that. We lit a fire, warmed ourselves and lay down. I found it difficult to sleep. I was tired; for days I had ridden long hours upon a rough camel, my body racked by its uneven gait. I suppose I was weak from hunger, for even by Bedu standards the food we ate was a starvation ration. But my thirst troubled me most. I was always conscious of it.

The others were awake at first light, anxious to push on. In a few minutes we were ready. We plodded along in silence. My eyes watered with the cold; the jagged salt-crusts cut and stung my feet. The world was grey and dreary. Then gradually the peaks ahead stood out against a paling sky; almost imperceptibly they began to glow, borrowing the colours of the sunrise that touched their crests.

## TOWERING DUNES

A high unbroken dune chain stretched across our front like a mountain range of peaks and connecting passes. Several of the summits seemed at least 700 feet above the salt flats on which we stood. The face that confronted us, being on the lee side to the prevailing wind, was very steep. Al Auf told us to wait and went forward to reconnoitre. I watched him climb up a ridge,

The harbour of Kuwait City, formerly Qurein, on the Persian Gulf, photographed by Captain Shakespear in 1913. Formerly under British protection, Kuwait achieved independence a year after this picture was taken, and was recognised by Britain as a sovereign state.

like a mountaineer struggling upward through soft snow, the only moving thing in all that empty landscape. I thought, 'God, we will never get the camels over that.' Some of them had lain down, an ominous sign. Bin Kabina sat beside me, cleaning the bolt of his rifle. I asked him, 'Will we ever get the camels over those dunes?' He pushed back his hair, looked at them, and said, 'Al Auf will find a way.' Al Auf came back, said, 'Come on,' and led us forward. It was now that he showed his skill, choosing the slopes up which the camels could climb. Very slowly, a foot at a time, we coaxed the unwilling beasts upward. Above us the rising wind was blowing streamers of sand. At last we reached the top. To my relief I saw we were on the edge of rolling dunes. I thought triumphantly, 'We have made it. We have crossed the Uruq al Shaiba.'

We went on, only stopping to feed at sunset. I said cheerfully to al Auf, 'Thank God we are across the Uruq al Shaiba.' He looked at me for a moment and answered, 'If we go well tonight we shall reach them tomorrow.' At first I thought he was joking. It was midnight when at last al Auf said, 'Let's stop here, get some sleep and give the camels a rest. The Uruq al Shaiba are not far away.' In my troubled dreams that night they towered above us, higher than the Himalayas.

Al Auf woke us while it was still dark. The morning star had risen above the dunes and formless things regained their shape in the dim light of dawn. We were faced by a range as high as the one we had crossed the day before, perhaps even higher, but here the peaks were steeper and more pronounced, many rising to great pinnacles down which the flowing ridges swept

like drapery. These sands, paler than those we had crossed, were very soft, cascading round our feet as the camels struggled up the slopes. It took us three hours to cross. From the summit we looked down to a salt flat in another great trough between the mountains. The range on the far side seemed even higher than the one on which we stood, and behind it were others. I thought, 'Our camels will never get up another of these awful dunes.' Yet somehow they did it. Then, utterly exhausted, we collapsed. Al Auf gave us a little water to wet our mouths. He said, 'We need this if we are to go on.' I pointed at the ranges ahead but he said, 'I can find a way between those; we need not cross them.' We went on till sunset, but now we were going with the grain of the land, no longer trying to climb the dunes – we could never have crossed another. We fed, got back on our camels and only stopped long after midnight; we started again at dawn.

## A GIFT FROM GOD

In the morning a hare jumped out of a bush: al Auf knocked it over with his stick. By three in the afternoon we could no longer resist stopping to cook it. Mabkhaut suggested, 'Let's roast it in its skin to save water.' Bin Kabina led the chorus of protest: 'No, by God, we don't want Mabkhaut's charred meat. We want soup. Soup and extra bread. We will feed well today. By God, I am hungry.' We were across the Uruq al Shaiba, and intended with this gift from God to celebrate the achievement.

As bin Kabina cooked the hare he looked across at me and said, 'The smell of this meat, Umbarak, makes me feel faint.'

A view of Mecca, looking northeast from the ridge west of the valley. The royal palace may be seen in the centre, across the encampment of pilgrims' tents. The photograph was taken in 1931 by St. J. B. Philby.

They divided the meat and then cast lots for the portions. Bedu generally do this; otherwise there are heated arguments, someone refusing to accept his portion, declaring he has been given more than his share. After we had taken it, bin Kabina said, 'I have forgotten to divide the liver. Give it to Umbarak.' After a show of protesting, I accepted it; I was too hungry to refuse. No Bedu would have done this.

Al Auf told us it would take three days to reach Khaba well in Dhafara, but that he knew of a very brackish well, nearer; the camels might drink its water. We rode again late into the night and there was a total eclipse of the moon. Again we started very early and rode for seven hours across rolling dunes. The colours of the sands were vivid, varied and unexpected, in places the colour of ground coffee, elsewhere brick-red, purple or a curious golden green.

Here we encountered Hamad bin Hanna, one of the sheiks of the Rashid. He was looking for a stray camel, but abandoned his search to come with us. He told us that Ibn Saud's tax collectors were in Dhafara, and advised us to avoid contact with the tribes, so that my presence would not get known. I had no desire to be arrested and taken off to explain my presence here to Ibn Jalawi, the formidable Governor of the Hassa. But we must at all costs avoid giving the impression that we were a raiding party, for honest travellers never pass an encampment without seeking news and food. It was going to be very difficult to escape detection.

Two days later we were at Khaba well, on the edge of Dhafara. The water here was only slightly brackish, delicious after the filthy, evil-smelling dregs that we had drunk the night before. We had passed another well but even our thirsty camels would not drink the bitter stuff. Here they drank bucketful after leathern bucketful. I have since heard of a test when a thirsty camel drank twenty-seven gallons.

## JOURNEY'S END

That night bin Kabina made extra coffee and Musallim increased our ration of flour by a mugful. This was wild extravagance, but even so the food he handed us was woefully inadequate to stay our hunger now that our thirst was gone. The moon was high above us when I lay down to sleep. The others talked around the fire, but I closed my mind to the meaning of their words, content only to hear the murmur of their voices, to watch their outline sharp against the moonlit sky, happily conscious that they were there, and beyond them the camels to which we owed our lives.

I had crossed the Empty Quarter. It was fourteen days since we had left the last well at Khaur bin Atarit. To others my journey would have little importance. It would produce nothing except a rather inaccurate map that no one was ever likely to use. It was a personal experience and the reward had been a drink of clean, tasteless water. I was content with that.

An undated photograph of a Turk with pistols and bared sword *(opposite)*. The Turks' warlike reputation goes back to the time of their ancestors, the Huns of Mongolia, who swept west and south from the third century onwards, terrorising all before them.

An early photograph dating from 1866, by A. Davis, showing the marketplace in Bethlehem (*above*). In the late nineteenth century Bethlehem was part of the Turkish Empire, but World War I put an end to 400 years of Turkish occupation. The Turks were driven out by the British who took over the administration of the region.

A house in Jedda, Hejaz, showing the typical *moucharaby* – projecting latticed windows – of Arab architecture (*opposite*). The photograph was taken in 1901 by L. Naretti and G. P. Devey, at a time when the Hejaz was a *vilayet* (province) of the Turkish empire.

Mosques, minarets, palaces and houses line the shore of the Bosphorus in this 1880 photograph of Istanbul, then called Constantinople, taken by R. H. Brown. This view shows the European side of the Bosphorus, including the Dolmabahçe Palace, built by the Turkish sultans on the promontory below St. Sophia. In 1880, Istanbul was the capital of the declining Ottoman Empire.

The famous surviving brick arch from the palace of the sixth-century King Chosroes at Ctesiphon near Baghdad, in a 1901 photograph presented to the Royal Geographical Society by Sir J. B. Goldsmid *(above)*. Ctesiphon was formerly the capital of the Sassanids, from AD 226.

The Mosque of Yeni-Velidé, Istanbul, photographed in about 1880 *(opposite)*. From the minarets of mosques such as this the Muslim call to prayer has rung out across the city for over 500 years.

Outsize neck chains link a group of prisoners at Birjand in eastern Iran (formerly Persia), in a photograph dating from 1903. Birjand lies in Khorasan province, close to the border with western Afghanistan. The whole region has a long history of conflict. The main ethnic group are the nomadic Chahar Aimaq.

In a photograph dated 1901 by L. Naretti and G. P. Devey, pilgrims pitch camp in Hejaz, now part of Saudi Arabia. In Hejaz lies the holy city of *Makkah* (Mecca), birthplace of the prophet Mohammed, which it is every Muslim's duty to visit once in his lifetime.

The English traveller and writer Freya Stark in Jebel ed Druz in southern
Syria, in 1928 (*above*). Born in 1893, Stark mastered Arabic and began her
journeys in the Middle East in 1927. A fearless explorer, she made solitary
journeys into such regions as Luristan, a mountainous province in western
Iran, and the Hadhramaut, a remote plateau in South Yemen. She recorded
her experiences in her photographs and prolific writings, notably *The
Valley of the Assassins* (1934), *The Southern Gates of Arabia* (1936) and *A
Winter in Arabia* (1940).

A street scene in Riyadh, formerly the capital of the sultanate of Nejd
*(opposite)*. The building furthest away has a crenellated parapet for defence,
and machiolation for pouring boiling oil onto attackers. The picture was
taken in 1937 by G. W. R. Rendel, just five years after Nejd merged with
Hejaz to form Saudi Arabia, with Riyadh as its capital.

A portrait of a young boy taken in 1947 in Saudi Arabia by Wilfred Thesiger *(opposite)*.

A photograph taken by Thesiger during his 1950-54 expedition to the Middle East, when he visited the marshlands of southern Iraq *(above left)*. The picture shows an early stage in the construction of a *mudhif*, a traditional building of the Marsh Arabs of the region. Construction begins with the formation of two rows of pillars made by binding together hundreds of the giant reeds that grow in the marshes. Each column may be as much as 2.4 metres (8 feet) in circumference.

The interior of a *mudhif*, from the same expedition, showing how the reed pillars have been joined at the top to form arches which are then infilled with reed matting *(above right)*. The *mudhifs* of each village serve as communal centres: it is here that the villagers gather socially, that visitors are shown hospitality, and that the elders meet.

The *mudhifs* of the Marsh Arabs lie in the vast marshes where the Tigris and Euphrates rivers join to flow into the Persian Gulf. In May the floodwaters are at their highest, as this photograph of a *mudhif* near the Hawr al Hammar lagoon shows. The humidity of the atmosphere in the marshes means that these giant reed constructions – as large as 15 metres (50 feet long) high and 4.6 metres (15 feet) wide – need rebuilding every ten years. The picture was taken by Wilfred Thesiger during his 1950-54 expedition.

Looking down from the ruins of an Arab castle to the tombs of the ancient city of Palmyra, in a photograph by Sir Peter Holmes *(opposite)*. Sited at an oasis in the Syrian desert approximately 240 kilometres (150 miles) northeast of Damascus, Palmyra was a flourishing city, but was destroyed by the Romans in AD 272 after an unsuccessful revolt led by its queen, Zenobia. Magnificent ruins remain, however. The village of Tadmur which stands at the site recalls Palmyra's Biblical name, Tadmor.

This photograph by Sir Peter Holmes shows the Ishak Paşa Sarayi, an eighteenth-century palace perched above the Ararat plain in Turkey *(above)*. From here the overlords of eastern Anatolia controlled the Silk Road below. The route is now the main highway between Turkey and Iran.

The sun lights the rock pools at Pamukkale in southwestern Turkey, in a picture by Chris Caldicott. On this elevated plateau, the terraces worn in the sulphurous rock have become natural reservoirs. Swimmers come to dip themselves in the salty waters, and the unusual nature of the site has placed Pamukkale on the tourist itinerary.

A view into Turkmenistan from the hills of northeastern Iran, photographed by Paul Harris in 1996. This is the traditional pastureland of the Turkoman. Once fully nomadic, most Turkoman now live a settled lifestyle, but some still follow the old ways for part of the year, forsaking their houses for tents and making brief migrations in search of grazing for their flocks of sheep and goats.

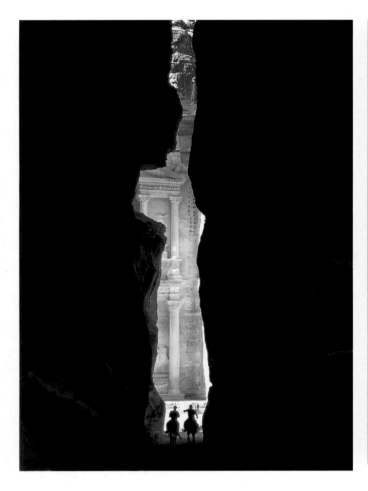 

The Siq, a long and increasingly narrow gorge, makes a dramatic entranceway to the ancient city of Petra, which can just be glimpsed in this picture taken by Chris Caldicott *(above left)*. Lying south of the Dead Sea in Jordan, the city was a Nabatean capital in the second century. Conquered by the Romans and later destroyed by Arabs, it lay forgotten for hundreds of years until it was rediscovered in 1812 by the Swiss traveller Johann Ludwig Burckhardt.

In a photograph by Patrick Syder, Bedu desert patrolmen wearing the red and white khaffiya and khaki uniform do guard duty at Petra *(above right)*.

A full view of one of the tombs known as the 'Treasury', the first building to greet the visitor on emergence from the Siq, photographed by Dr Stephen Coyne *(opposite)*. Famously described by the poet John Burgon as 'a rose-red city – half as old as Time', Petra is carved from red sandstone.

The ancient town of Habban, photographed in the late evening sun by Patrick Syder. Habban was formerly the Jewish centre of Yemen, which lies on the historic trading route between Asia and Africa, just south of Saudi Arabia. The Sephardim – the branch of Jews who spread south into Arabia and east into Asia from Palestine during the centuries of the Jewish diaspora – found Islam at that time a more tolerant regime than the Christianity of Europe.

Looking out from the peak of Mount Aretain, a dormant volcano in
northeastern Jordan, across the *badia* – desert – that covers much of the
country. The picture was taken in 1996 by Chris Caldicott during the
Jordan Badia Research and Development Programme, set up by the Royal
Geographical Society in collaboration with the Jordanian administration.

A view from the dunes of the Wahiba Sands across the valley of the Wadi Al Batha in Oman, shortly after a heavy rainstorm *(above)*. The photograph was taken in 1986 by Nigel Winser, leader of the Oman Wahiba Sands Project of 1985–87, organised by the Royal Geographical Society and the Omani government. The purpose of the Project was to study the geomorphology of the sand sea and its ecosystem, and to assess the impact of change on its inhabitants.

The rock palace of Dar al-Hajar at Wadi Dhahr near Sana'a in Yemen, photographed by Chris Bradley in 1990 *(opposite)*. Located on the site of an earlier settlement, this traditional stone-built house was constructed as a summer palace for Iman Yahya in the 1930s.

Australasia

# uncharted southlands

## Christina Dodwell

THE ORIGINAL DISCOVERERS OF Australasia were the prehistoric adventurers and migrant peoples who travelled out from the Asian mainland during the last Ice Age.

As the glaciers grew, peoples retreated from them, pushing and displacing other communities down towards the coast, until emigration across the ocean was the best option. Prehistoric artefacts indicate that, by AD 300, some emigrants had reached Samoa, the Marquesas and Tahiti.

The first recorded contact between Europe and Southeast Asia was in mediaeval times, when Marco Polo was returning to Europe from China in the thirteenth century, travelling by sea past the Malay Peninsula and reaching Sumatra, where the boat was held up for five months by adverse weather. In his journal of 1292, Marco Polo records his visits throughout Sumatra, and information about other islands. Arab seafarers who stopped at ports on Java's north coast (they never saw the south) believed it was the largest island in the world.

Around the same time, a number of Franciscan friars travelled deep into Asia, often also returning by sea through Southeast Asia and writing a number of books about their travels. One of the finest mediaeval travel-writers was Varthema of Bologna who spent several years in Southeast Asia and whose first book was published in 1510 in Latin, English, French, German, Spanish and Dutch.

By the early 1600s, several European countries had established trading posts in Southeast Asia: the East India Company, for example, was formed in 1599 to bring tea and spices from the region to England. Trade was highly competitive: each season's crop brought a crowd of vessels to the region's ports, all attempting to outdo each other in loading up and getting home as fast as possible. (In records at the House of Dodwell in Hong Kong, I read about a captain who was in such a hurry to catch the tide that, rather than allowing the pilot's boat to be brought alongside for him to disembark in the usual way, simply threw him overboard.)

### AN IMAGINARY CONTINENT

All this meant that Southeast Asia was well known to Europeans as long as 500 years ago, though seafarers did not venture further than the lucrative Spice Islands. The lands beyond were hostile and seemed to offer no easy pickings, and the ships had poor navigation equipment. But the demands of trade were relentless, and further exploration followed. Much more lay awaiting discovery further south: Australia, New Zealand, New Guinea and the archipelagos of Oceania and the South Pacific.

Rumours of a great continent in the South Seas persisted in Europe throughout the centuries. It was thought logical that there must be a great southern landmass, to balance the already known continents and coasts of Europe, Asia, Africa and eastern America. This vast south land was referred to as *terra australis incognita* ('the unknown land in the south') – what we now call Australia is only a fraction of the landmass they believed existed.

Various adventurers searched for this imaginary southern continent: in 1567 there was the Spaniard Mendana, and his compatriot Quiros; the Dutchmen Lemaire and

Harvesting wheat at Cannings Down station near Warwick, Queensland, photographed in the 1890s by J.P. Thomson. Large-scale wheat production in Australia began in the 1860s; by the end of the century the amount of land devoted to wheat farming had increased fivefold.

Schouten in 1615; Tasman in 1639; the Frenchman Bougainville, who set out the same year as the Briton, Wallis in 1766; followed by Dampier, Cook, Bligh, and others.

The history of first contact was seldom happy. The initial meeting of Mendana and his crew with the people of the Marquesas left 200 islanders dead after a fight, and infected many others with syphilis. The ship's next call was at Santa Cruz, where the massacre carried out by the crew was worse. Mendana executed the ringleaders and, in doing so, provoked a mutiny. By the end of the year Mendana's old and battered ship had sunk and he and most of his crew were dead from sickness and starvation. Most expeditions were failures; not only failing to find the southern continent, also failing to re-find islands they had previously discovered. But they named and claimed whatever they found.

The sailors who arrived on an island were hungry, ruthless soldiers of fortune. They lived among rats and filth on long voyages. Their food for weeks could be flour mixed with salt-water and baked in ashes; and liquid intake was rationed to a once-daily half pint of stinking water. Every day, a dead man was thrown overboard. They were unlikely to be sympathetic to the peoples whose communities they came upon.

For the islanders, being 'discovered' meant that armed foreigners took official possession of the island and planted a flag on the beach as a signal of their invasion. But the islanders were not docile victims. Their instinct was to protect their territory and there was frequent bloodshed. Battle was not new to them: their own wars often involved human sacrifice and cannibalism.

In New Zealand the ferocity of the Maoris, who attacked most landing parties, made first contact difficult. Captain Cook sought friendship with the Maori chiefs by kidnapping some Maoris and offering them gifts and hospitality. The tactic failed.

During Cook's time this great age of European sea exploration developed into a new style of state-funded expedition with scientific and political motives. The invention of improved navigational equipment in the mid-1700s made it possible to plot courses and chart islands with reasonable accuracy.

THE FINAL AGE OF MARITIME DISCOVERY

Cook was a dedicated discoverer with a passion for scientific precision. His 1768 voyage, to find the 'southern continent' and to record the transit of the planet Venus in Tahiti, set a precedent by having a full complement of scientists on board: astronomers, chart-makers, naturalists and artists. Among them was Sir Joseph Banks, who expanded the idea of scientific observation into exploration in his study of nature and people's customs, while the islanders, in their turn, observed the foreigners. This final age of British maritime discovery lasted only while ships were available. When the American War of Independence broke out, the ships were needed elsewhere.

Australia is geologically the oldest of continents, having been a landmass a billion years ago. The Aborigines are a distinct race, not related to neighbouring peoples, though their physique resembles pre-historic aboriginal fossils from Java. This supports the theory they were an early tribe that was pushed out of pre-glacial Asia, and forced to re-migrate from Java.

Rawkawa Falls on the Mangawhero River, New Zealand, North Island, photographed in the 1900s by A.S. Waley. The Mangawhero has its source at Mount Ruapehu, an active volcano and now a popular resort.

Some of the early naval expeditions knew parts of the Australian coast, but did not realise it was a continent. The fertile east shore was not charted until Cook arrived in 1770. But by 1787, the transportation of convicts to Australia was already under way.

In 1801 a British sailor, Captain Matthew Flinders, circumnavigated the coast, and in 1840 Edward Eyre led the first expedition across the continent from east to west. In his contact with Aborigines, Eyre was sympathetic, and he had an appreciation of their culture. He also recorded natural wonders, as in the approach to the dome of Ayers Rock, and the extraordinary termite-nest spires and pinnacles on flat plains.

Eyre's journey was only the beginning. An impressive number of Gold Medals have been awarded by the Royal Geographical Society for Australian exploration: Eyre, Strezelecki, Stuart, Brooke, Burke and Wills (who died after traversing Australia), Gregory, Warburton, Forrest, Giles and Thomson all contributed to charting the interior of Australia.

Later explorers paid attention to the peoples and the natural history of the lands they explored. Beatrice Grimshaw, a little-known nineteenth-century explorer, spent a month on Malekula (now part of Vanuatu) and wrote about the drum-idols and death masks there, and the headbinding of children to make their skulls conical. Among Beatrice's adventures was a trek up the spitting volcano at Tanna Island, where one can stand on the crater rim and watch the heaving red abyss beneath. She also made several underwater dives, using a heavy old-fashioned suit and helmet with hose-pipe air-line.

Most women who travelled through the South Pacific at this time were less energetic. Evelyn Cheeseman, one of the greatest of Victorian women explorers, spent twelve years collecting insects in the South Seas. Few careers were open to women at that time. Evelyn chose entomology, became an insect-keeper at London Zoo and was invited to join a zoological expedition to the Pacific in early 1900s. After this she spent a year in Malekula and another in New Guinea, where she was respected by the apparently fearsome people, approaching them with courtesy and a genuine interest in learning. She brought home 42,000 insects, many new to science, and was awarded an OBE, but is now almost forgotten.

### DISCOVERING THE GARDEN OF EDEN

The discovery of the interior of New Guinea did not take place until comparatively recently, in the 1930s. The New Guinea coasts were known by then, and had attracted settlers who had started coconut plantations.

Prospectors for gold had made dazzling finds in the south east part of the island. But the interior was assumed to be entirely made up of a harsh, cold, wet mountain range. Then, in the early years of the 1930s, two strong and bright-natured Australian prospectors, Michael Leahy and Michael Dwyer, made the first exploratory patrol. The results of this and their subsequent patrols, which found the entrance to the Wahgi Valley, were surprising to everyone.

There was not one solid mountain interior but two long ranges enclosing a lost world of temperate hilly grasslands

On the summit of Mount Tutoho, New Zealand. The mountain, 2756 metres (9045 ft) high, was first climbed on the 24th of March 1924 by Peter Graham and Samuel Turner.

and fertile valleys. Its mild climate was like eternal spring, with no mosquitoes, making it a Garden of Eden. It was neatly farmed with an abundance of yams, taro, beans, and sugarcane planted in straight rows, with drainage ditches and stockaded homes. It was a Stone Age culture: the people were naked except for a loincloth of bark fibre and a bunch of leaves behind, and in their hair the men wore feathers from Birds of Paradise.

Because exploration took place so recently, there are a number of photographs and films of the first contact between the highlanders and outsiders. The two groups of people were equally interesting to each other: the highlanders were fascinated by the modern equipment the newcomers owned, especially when a patrol took a gramophone along with them.

## Tracing a Route

In 1980, after three months on the mainland of Southeast Asia, I set out along a route that followed that of some of the first travellers and explorers in the region. First, I went down the Malay Peninsula during the rituals of Thaipusam, island-hopping through Indonesia, and going to ceremonies of offerings and of cremation. I enjoyed the events, the music of gamelan orchestras, and richly-decorated temples set beside curved terraces of glittering rice paddies, but I could not help thinking that tourism has replaced discovery.

From Java I caught a cargo boat heading east and set up my camp on deck alongside many families of pioneers, on their way to settle in new homes in Timor and Irian Jaya (the eastern part of the island of New Guinea). This was a transmigration scheme sponsored by the Indonesian government and my companions were mostly peasant farming families pushed into emigration from Java by pressure of a population of 80 million. Some of them still believe Java is the world's largest island, though one who knew the truth said he had been quite shocked to realise how small Java really is.

At Kupang the ship also took on 800 head of cattle, loaded on to the decks and into the holds, to deliver to this and last years' emigrants. I had to move camp off the deck on to the prow, and hung my hammock between a winch and a bale of rope. The voyage lasted nearly a month.

The cattle were delivered to their new owners in Timor and Irian Jaya by slinging them off the ship in rope nets, one beast for each family. I disembarked at Jayapura, the last port of call. No boats went on from there.

Following this, in 1990, I travelled on an ocean research boat in the South Pacific, among the Vanuatu islands where Mendana's ship had sunk. The evidence was of more recent conflict. I looked at the wrecks left from World War II; and at a crashed warplane lying in a forgotten jungle. I saw beaches littered with rusted naval landing craft and artillery, and found on another beach a tidy row of rusty tanks.

Our research boat was fitted out for scuba diving. I did some trial dives on coral reefs then went down forty metres to the wreck of the American warship *President Coolidge*. The ship was carrying troops when it hit a mine and sank. Rifles and helmets lie abandoned on the decks, adding to the eeriness of this spectacular underwater exploration.

Camels in South Australia, photographed by V.C. Scott O'Connor in the 1920s. Camels were imported into Australia in the mid-nineteenth century and were a valuable means of transport in desert areas until the 1940s.

On the nearby island of Malekula the Nambas tribes still follow many of their ancient traditions. My guide wore a banana leaf penis sheath and, as we trekked inland through forest, we came to a 'living stone' where dead bodies had rotted to set their spirits free, and their empty skulls stared blankly into the forest. We were going to see a celebration of the afterlife, being held in a swept clearing bordered with ornamental shrubs and great upright wooden slit drum-idols. From the column of dancers came a rising chant and rhythm of feet in a vigorous display to attract the goodwill of their ancestors.

## A Curiosity

Even today, parts of Papua New Guinea are rarely visited by outsiders. Trekking there for a year, I was treated more as a novelty than a threat: in remote parts I was often the first white woman people had seen. Arriving at huts, I would shake hands with the men, then with the women, who in turn wanted me to touch their babies – who screamed in terror.

In the southern and western highlands of Papua New Guinea the men I met wore great wigs of human hair, everyday wigs decorated with bits of ferns, and special wigs more ornate with wonderful plumes from Birds of Paradise. Face painting was also common, and nose decoration, be it a straw or a pig's tusk slotted through their nose.

A few years after that journey, I went back to Papua New Guinea, in fact to the Wahgi Valley, to do a BBC Television film including a rafting expedition down the Wahgi River. It was to be a first descent into untrodden territory. I could understand why, when I saw their video, filmed from a light aircraft. It showed the steep, rocky, forested mountains and raging white-water river. The Wahgi villagers turned out in feathered finery to give us a send-off.

One of our three rafts turned upside-down in rapids on the first day, injuring the people on it. Each day the river grew more ferocious; my raft overturned in rapids a few days later, and shortly afterwards the other raft capsized in a giant eddy.

At this point, the television crew decided they had had enough and we pulled out. None of this was quite my idea of exploration, though there were some special moments camping on river banks and bathing in waterfalls in unnamed rocky tributaries. Not far from the valley, on a separate expedition, I trekked to an overhang in the forested limestone crags where corpses dating from the 1940s were sitting in wicker baskets in a row against the cliff. Smoke-dried and lightweight, their skin was like parchment.

Looking back on my own and other explorers' journeys, I am struck by how the meaning of discovery has evolved. Once essential to trade and the drive to expand territory, it became equally important to science. Astronomy was developed through exploration, as was navigation, then botany and ethnology. Today, the emphasis is more often on learning to care for peoples and their environments.

Two Aboriginals in the 1890s *(opposite)*. Violence, disease and loss of resources led to a population fall of ninety percent among some Aboriginal groups within twenty years of their first meeting with Europeans.

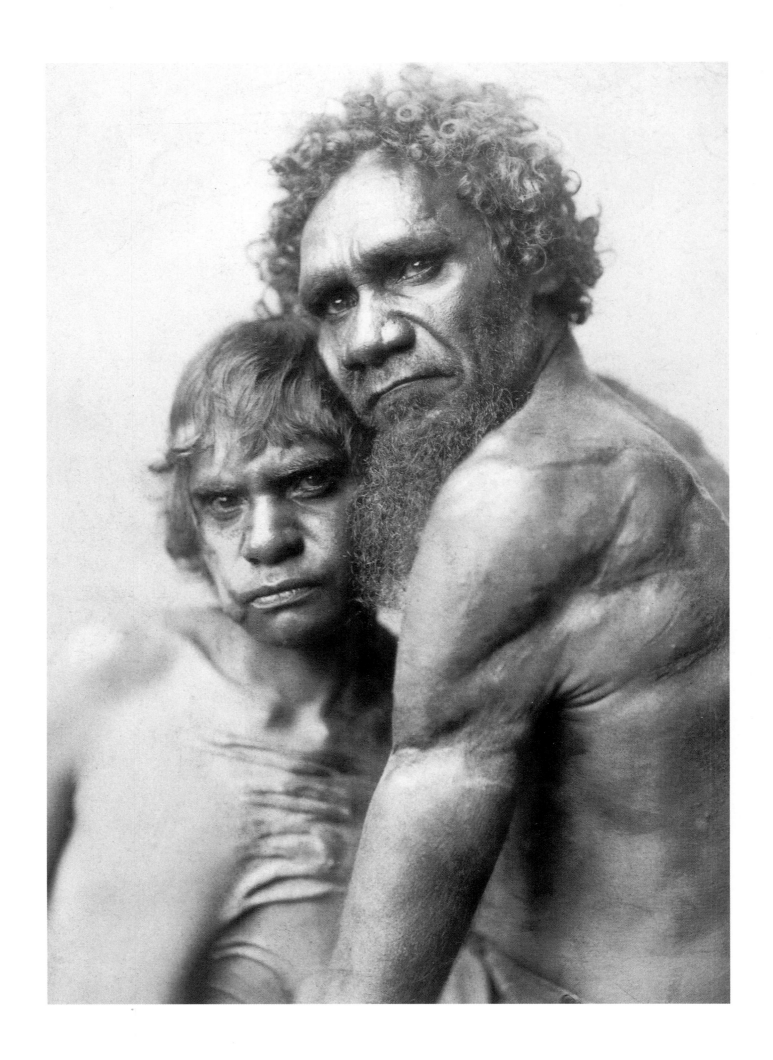

237

A Chinese funeral in Cooktown, Queensland in the 1890s. The port of Cooktown served the nearby goldfields and, during the goldrush of the 1870s, a Chinese community many thousands strong grew up in both the fields and in the town itself. By the time this picture was taken, output had declined and many diggers had left.

The Custom House, Wellington, New Zealand in the 1890s. At the time this picture was taken Wellington had been in existence only about fifty years, having been chosen in 1839 as a site for a port by its founder, Edward Gibbon Wakefield. It became the country's capital in 1865. The city was named after the Duke of Wellington, who had supported and encouraged its foundation.

'Drum–idols', statues representing ancestral spirits in the form of tall drums, in Vanuatu. This photograph *(above left)* was taken by Melbourne-based photographer, W.J. Lindt, who travelled among the islands, then called the New Hebrides, in the early 1890s.

A second photograph by W.J. Lindt shows recruiting ships visiting Vanuatu in the 1890s *(above right)*. In the second half of the nineteenth century, there was widespread 'recruitment' of labour from the islands of the Pacific to the cotton and sugar plantations of Australia, Fiji and Samoa, where working conditions were often appalling. The practice was known as 'blackbirding' and up to a quarter of the labourers who ended up on the plantations were there as a result of being tricked, misled or coerced.

Boatbuilders on the island of Épi, Vanuatu, in the 1890s, also photographed by W.J. Lindt *(opposite)*. The people of Vanuatu are Melanesians, whose traditional boats are dug-out canoes, each one skilfully carved from the trunk of a single tree.

A chief in Samoa, in the 1900s (*above*). This group of islands is home to the largest group of Polynesians after the Maoris of New Zealand. Even today, Samoan society remains traditional in structure. The basic unit of society is an extended family group, made up of blood relations and others who have been adopted into it. This grouping, known as an *aiga*, is headed by an elected chief, or *matai*.

Maori people bathing by a waterfall on Rarotonga, the most heavily populated of the Cook Islands, in the late 1890s, while Europeans look on (*opposite*). The Maoris had been living in the Cook Islands for hundreds of years by the time Europeans arrived in the early nineteenth century. From that time until the 1890s, the government of the islands was largely by missionaries from the London Missionary Society.

Log hauling by bullock team, photographed in the 1920s. Large areas of Australia's forests have been cleared since the arrival of the first European settlers, in order to open up land for farming. Indiscriminate logging in the past has led to the drastic reduction of some native species of trees.

Sheep-shearing in Queensland in the 1900s. Wool has been a major export from Australia since the 1820s, and was produced in Queensland from the 1840s onwards. Successive settlers occupied more and more land with their sheep, dispossessing the original inhabitants, the Aborigines. Sheep farming is not normally labour intensive, but shearing is. The task became easier from the late 1880s, when Frederick Wolseley revolutionised the industry with the invention of mechanised shears.

A Maori chief, photographed in the early 1900s *(above left)*. He wears a fur cloak (possibly dogskin, which was much valued by high-ranking men), and his face is decorated with tattoos, known as *moko*, in patterns of spirals and curved lines. Tattooing was carried out using a sharp bone blade dipped in a mix of soot and water. It was extremely painful and had to be done a little at a time.

Like the man on the left, this Maori woman *(above right)* was also photographed in the 1900s. She wears a feather cloak, known as a *kahu huruhuru*. Both portraits serve as a record of traditional Maori dress and customs. The Maoris settled in New Zealand from Pacific islands to the north, where the climate was warm. There, their traditional clothing had been made from bark-cloth, but this proved too cold in their new southern home and alternatives were found.

Maori women cooking food and boiling kettles in steam holes in Rotorua, on the North Island of New Zealand in the early 1900s. Until the end of the nineteenth century, the region was inhabited almost entirely by Maoris, but from the 1880s onwards, a township grew up to cater for tourists attracted by the hot springs. In contrast to the two people shown opposite, these women wear Western dress. They are also using Western cooking utensils.

Bondi Beach, New South Wales in 1920 *(above)*. Bondi, now one of the most famous surfing beaches in the world, was already a popular resort when this photograph was taken. Australia's first surf lifesaving club was formed at Bondi Beach in 1907. Surfboard riding was introduced to Australia in 1915.

A canoe in the Santa Cruz Islands, now part of the Solomon Islands *(opposite)*. The canoe is Polynesian, with an outrigger, and a superstructure built between this and the main hull. Much larger, ocean-going outrigger canoes had been used previously, when Polynesians travelled thousands of kilometres across the Pacific to settle on distant islands.

A *tiki*, or free-standing carved figure, in a photograph taken in 1923 *(opposite)*. While the heads of such figures were often freely interpreted, many, like this one, were realistic enough to show the patterns of facial tattoo *(moko)*. The patterns on this figure's face echo those on the face of the Maori chief shown on page 246. The word *tiki* is also used to describe small greenstone figures worn around the neck.

The old meets the new: people in Papua New Guinea in the 1930s listen to a gramophone for the first time *(above)*. Two Australian prospectors, Michael Leahy and Michael Dwyer, travelled extensively in the highlands of Papua New Guinea at this time and a gramophone was among the modern pieces of equipment they brought with them. It was, not surprisingly, a source of fascination to people who until that time had had little or no contact with the outside world.

A village on Ontong Java (formerly known as Lord Howe Atoll) in the Solomon Islands. The picture was taken in the 1890s by C.M. Woodford who, as Acting Deputy Commissioner for the Solomons, made tours of inspection among the islands to assess their 'prospects and resources'. He concluded that the islands were especially suited to growing coconut palms, which suggested that copra (the dried kernel of the coconut, used to yield coconut oil) was the best crop for export. In addition to being a source of income, the coconut palm provided building materials. People thatched the roofs of their homes with palm leaves and made walls from panels of woven leaves.

Middle Harbour, Sydney, on the road from Manly to the Spit, around 1909. The photograph was taken for the Agent General of Australia, which indicates it was meant to be used for publicity purposes. The Agent General's job was to work in London as a commercial and emigration agent, promoting commerce and tourism.

A man from the Mount Hagen area of Papua New Guinea, in the early 1930s *(above)*. This picture was taken by Michael Leahy on one of several journeys into the New Guinea highlands. He and his companion Michael Dwyer were struck by what they called the 'adornments' of the highlanders, which included headdresses of feathers and ferns, in addition to other decorations such as bones or pig tusks through the septum. The cowrie shells of the necklace were used as a form of currency.

The practice of binding a child's head so that it developed, in adulthood, into the conical shape shown here was traditionally carried out in parts of New Guinea *(opposite)*. This photograph was taken in the 1930s.

A modern photograph by Edward Mendell of a Huli man from the southern highlands of Papua New Guinea *(opposite)*. He is dressed for a wedding at which he has been a guest. In addition to a decorated wig, which is part of his normal dress, he wears also feathers, beads and face paint, in honour of this special occasion.

A Dani warrior from the highlands of Irian Jaya (the eastern part of the island of New Guinea) wearing a traditional penis gourd *(above left)*. Gourds like this, made from the dried shell of a member of the pumpkin family, are worn most of the time by Dani men and are virtually their only clothing. In order to keep warm in what is quite a cool climate, they often smear themselves with pig fat. The photograph is by Adrian Arbib.

Photographed in 1991 by Paul Harris, this Polynesian woman's clothing contrasts dramatically with that of the Dani warrior *(above right)*. She is traditionally dressed; in this case for her daughter's wedding. Her clothing is made from tapa, a cloth made from the bark of trees such as the wild fig, breadfruit or paper mulberry.

A tiny plant pushes its way through the sands of Australia's Gibson Desert, which stretches over much of Central Australia. This photograph by Joann Crowther was taken near Ayers Rock, in the Northern Territory. Some of the largest sand dunes in the world are found in this region, where rainfall is extremely rare. When it does rain, seeds that have been lying dormant, often for years, spring almost instantly into life.

New Zealand's young, volcanic landscape, with its high mountains, boiling mud pools and hot water springs, draws tourists from all over the world. This photograph by Chris Wright shows steam rising from a pool of hot thermal water, which has been dramatically coloured by mineral deposits from the rocks around it.

the Americas

# new worlds

## Dr. John Hemming

THE EXPLORATION OF THE AMERICAS is full of paradoxes. First, there are the names. Amerigo Vespucci (1454-1512), after whom the two continents were named, was the most successful 'travel writer' of his day. Florentine by birth and formerly a merchant in the service of Lorenzo de' Medici, Vespucci made several voyages across the Atlantic, sometimes under the Spanish flag, sometimes the Portuguese, spurred by the desire to find a western trade route to the Indian Ocean and its Spice Islands. On his third expedition in 1501, with a Portuguese fleet, Vespucci reached the coast of Brazil. When his often exaggerated account of the voyage was published, it caused such a sensation that a cartographer in Lorraine christened the newly discovered southern continent after him — *Americi Terra vel America* — somewhat unfairly, however, since Columbus had first arrived in the region nearly a decade earlier.

In discovering this new land, Columbus firmly believed that he had found the fabled India of which Marco Polo had spoken. As a consequence of this adamant belief, two further misnomers arose: the natives of both South and North America were named 'Indians' and the Caribbean islands were called the 'West Indies'.

### ILLUSION OF YOUTH

The aura of newness and youth that has been and is still attached to the 'New World' — or Mundus Novus as Vespucci wrote in a letter to Lorenzo de' Medici — is also misleading. There is nothing new about land masses that contain, in Canada's Laurentian shield or South America's Guiana shield, the most ancient precambrian rocks to be seen anywhere on earth. Nor is there any novelty in the many fossils and dinosaur remains excavated everywhere from Alberta to Patagonia. These ancient tectonic plates are 'new' only to mankind and to Europeans. Human beings migrated from Asia to North America during the recent pleistocene ice age between 20,000 and 10,000 years ago, and Europeans arrived and settled there only after 1492.

The pattern of European discovery continued for longer there than in other parts of the world. The Americas were explored and mapped far earlier than Africa, Australia or central Asia. The conquistador Vasco Núñez de Balboa crossed the isthmus of Panama and laid claim to what he called the 'South Sea' — or Pacific Ocean — as early as 1513; and only five years later Fernão Magalhães (or Ferdinand Magellan) found a passage around the south of South America before going on to explore the Pacific coast and prepare for the first circumnavigation of the earth. Francisco de Orellana descended the entire length of the world's greatest river, the Amazon, in 1542 — almost 350 years before Burton and Speke solved the mystery of the source of the Nile. By the end of the sixteenth century, the length of the Andes and most of Mexico and Central America were thoroughly known; and in the next century the Mississippi and Saint Lawrence were well mapped. Indians showed Samuel de Champlain, Louis Jolliet, René de la Salle and other French *voyageurs* how to paddle up rivers and lakes into the heart of North America. British fur traders and explorers were equally adventurous. In 1789 Alexander Mackenzie followed the river later named after him as far as the Arctic Ocean, and three years

The Niagara Falls in the 1860s. The falls lie on the border between the United States and Canada, formerly 'New France', and are part of the network of lakes and waterways which opened the way into the interior for such explorer-adventurers as Jacques Cartier, Samuel de Champlain and Robert Cavelier de la Salle.

later he completed the first crossing of the continent. In 1804-6, Lewis and Clark followed the Missouri to its source, crossed the Rockies at their widest point and also reached the Pacific shore. Soon afterwards, Simon Fraser, David Thompson and Hugh Palliser surveyed unknown parts of the Canadian Rockies. In contrast to the pattern of American exploration, the Congo and Niger had to wait until the late nineteenth century for their European discoverers.

## ACROSS THE ROOF OF THE WORLD

Another paradox about American exploration is that it lost its early lead. By 1830, when the Royal Geographical Society was founded, the greatest blank on the outline of the world map was the North-West Passage – the sea route between the Atlantic and Pacific Oceans around the top of North America – and the islands north of Canada. And today Amazonia, which has some of the world's richest biological diversity, is still the location for discoveries of hundreds of species of new flora and fauna and occasionally even of tribal people. Africa, by contrast, is fully explored. During almost 170 years since the Royal Geographical Society was founded, exploration in the Americas has concentrated on these two wilderness regions.

In 1845 the British Admiralty sent two sail-steamers commanded by the veteran polar explorer and vice-president of the RGS, Sir John Franklin, to find a passage through the ice-bound and desolate labyrinth of islands of the Canadian Arctic. The ships and their men were last seen by a whaler off Baffin Island later that year. Total silence followed. As the years went by,

the increasing distress felt by the RGS and others was voiced in the annual speeches of the Society's presidents. Relief expeditions were sent, some by sea and others by land. Reports by Eskimos (Inuit) of a column of forty starving men marching south, and a message about Franklin's death were received; some graves and a few other relics were found. But most of the men and the two ships have never reappeared and, to this day, expeditions are still searching for traces of the greatest calamity in the annals of British exploration.

The blanks in the map of northern Canada were filled in during the ensuing century. Dr John Rae used Inuit methods to explore overland, while others traversed the great north-flowing Canadian rivers, and gold prospectors poured into the Klondike and Yukon. In 1875 another Admiralty expedition, closely linked to the Royal Geographical Society, explored the north coast of Ellesmere Island and got farther north than any previous attempt.

The final triumphs came in the early years of this century. In 1903-6, the Norwegian Roald Amundsen and six companions finally took a tiny motorised sailing ship from east to west through the North-West Passage. The race was also on to reach the North Pole. In 1909, the flamboyant American Commander Robert Peary achieved this goal, boasting, 'The Pole at last! The prize of three centuries. My dream and goal for twenty years. Mine at last!' Some scholars would contest this statement, however, maintaining that the honour belonged to Peary's unassuming compatriot Dr Frederick Cook, who claimed to have reached the Pole a year earlier. In the five years

On the 'playa' on the Peruvian coast. Lying between the Andes and the Pacific Ocean's cold Humboldt Current, Peru's coastal strip has a desert climate. The picture, dating from between 1910 and 1913, was taken along the route of the southern railway.

from 1913 to 1918, the gallant Canadian Vilhjamur Stefansson surveyed the remainder of the northernmost islands, in a series of harrowing expeditions.

## SOUTHWARD-BOUND
In 1831, the year after the foundation of the RGS, the Royal Navy sent HMS Beagle to chart the coasts of the other extremity of the Americas. The five-year voyage achieved fame because the Beagle's captain Robert Fitzroy took his young friend Charles Darwin to keep him company. Having surveyed the shores of Chile, the ship then mapped the Galápagos Islands. Here, Darwin noticed that the beaks of the finches on each island varied slightly, being adapted to the local habitat and food supply, and it was this that inspired his explosive theory of evolution by natural selection.

More recently, the great Himalayan mountaineer Eric Shipton explored the mountains of Tierra del Fuego – now named the Cordillera Darwin, overlooking the Beagle Channel. Farther north in the Andes, Clements Markham (later to be a famous president of the RGS) and other travellers marvelled at the monuments of the Incas. But it was a young American, Hiram Bingham, who in 1911 discovered the most spectacular ruin in all the Americas – the lost city of Machu Picchu.

Throughout this period, Amazonia was the region which attracted most explorers and naturalists. The vast basin of the Amazon, by far the world's largest river, contains the majority of the earth's tropical rainforests and its richest biodiversity. German, French and Brazilian scientists have identified many of Amazonia's flora, fauna and native peoples. The Brazilian explorer and humanitarian Candido Rondon discovered and surveyed more rivers, tribes and territory than any other explorer, during the decades between 1880 and 1920. The greatest scientific impact, though, was made by three young British naturalists. Alfred Russell Wallace, Henry Walter Bates and Richard Spruce all reached the Amazon in 1848 and spent many years making immense collections and discovering hundreds of new species on the river and its major tributaries. Bates went on to be the first paid Secretary of the Royal Geographical Society, and the RGS helped Wallace to reach Southeast Asia, where he further developed Darwin's theory.

## EXPEDITIONS IN THE RAINFOREST
I myself have been in unexplored parts of the Amazon forests during four periods of my life. The first was a six-month expedition to explore and map the headwaters of the Iriri River in central Brazil. I experienced many of the joys and thrills of exploration – discovering, surveying and naming hitherto unknown rivers and waterfalls; cutting kilometres of trails in the certain knowledge that no non-Indian had ever trodden there; suddenly encountering tapir, jaguar, brocket deer, peccary and other forest fauna; and living in hammocks in the comforting gloom of the forest, with all its beauty and natural marvels.

But we also endured the same hardships as other explorers. There was the physical exhaustion of hacking through tough and tangled undergrowth, frequently without water, and carrying heavy packs of supplies for day after day across the

Los Angeles in about 1929, seen from Mount Wilson Observatory, 1710 metres (5700 feet) above sea level. Beyond the city lies the vast expanse that explorer Vasco Nuñez de Balboa dubbed the 'South Sea', what we now know as the Pacific Ocean.

uneven and often swampy forest floor. We ate whatever we could hunt or gather, but we were working hard and the lack of food was an ugly experience that I shall never forget. At times the forest was high, with magnificent trees towering over thirty metres (100 feet) above us, their canopies linked in a tracery of lianes. This meant that the forest floor was relatively open. Being only eleven men in a limitless expanse of unexplored country, we were often alone and it was easy to stray from our rudimentary path across the carpet of roots and dead leaves. I vividly recall the panic whenever I found myself lost in this way, knowing that unless I rediscovered the trail or a blaze on a tree, I could disappear forever into the wilderness.

As the weeks went by, we moved our camps forward and then spent many days cutting two dugout canoes and their pole-paddles, only to discover after further exploration that we were on the wrong river. It took an agonizing effort of will for our weary team to press ahead across a watershed and build more canoes on the Iriri. We emerged thin, pale from weeks without seeing the sun, and covered in insect bites and festering scratches. Just as we were about to embark on the first descent of the unexplored Iriri, the expedition leader, my close friend Richard Mason, was killed. Unknown Indians laid an ambush on our main trail, and killed Richard with arrows and a blow from a club that crushed his head. It was several days before we could embalm the body and carry it back to the isolated Cachimbo airstrip and eventual burial in the British cemetery in Rio de Janeiro. We later learned that the killers were a long-range hunting party from the Amazonian Kren-Akrore (or Panará)

tribe, with whom Europeans only made peaceful contact a decade after the ambush.

This tragic encounter with a hitherto-unknown group of Indians inspired me to learn more about the indigenous peoples of Amazonia. I spent two years with native tribes, visiting over forty groups in all stages of acculturation, from first contact to assimilation into frontier society. The most exciting moments were seeing four tribes at the time of their very first experience of outside society. I was with teams from the Brazilian Indian foundation, who had often taken years of exploration to arrive at the moment of face-to-fact contact. They did this by leaving presents of knives, beads and other manufactured goods. Metal axes and machetes have an irresistible appeal to men who spend weeks clearing forest with stone tools. One new group that I saw, the Suruí in Rondônia, were highly suspicious of us, doubtless because they had had murderous contact with frontier settlers or prospectors. Only the warriors came to the Brazilian attraction post, and they were never without their bows and arrows.

A month after I left that attraction post, something went wrong. The Suruí overran the place, killing the few Brazilians who were there. Two other tribes whom I saw immediately after first contact, the Parakanã of Pará and the Galera Nambikwara of Rondônia, were in a state of shock, traumatised by the awesome experience of their first encounter with an alien civilisation. But a fourth group, the Asurini who live in the forests between the Xingú and Tocantins Rivers, were people of seemingly boundless goodness and innocence, who

A photograph of Cuzco, once the Inca capital, showing the colonial church of San Sebastián. It was taken in 1932 by Professor J. W. Gregory on his last expedition. Gregory drowned while negotiating the Urubamba River.

welcomed us almost as visiting deities. During my brief time with the Asurini, I understood why Vespucci and other early explorers regarded Brazilian Indians as noble savages living in a terrestrial paradise. I have been fortunate enough to see more tribes than any other non-Brazilian, and my contacts with these remarkable people, often living in a pre-Stone Age, were an unforgettable experience.

## SCIENTIFIC ACHIEVEMENTS

The finest discoveries are now made by scientists unravelling the mysteries of Amazonia's complex ecology. I participated in a Venezuelan expedition to the unexplored table mountains on that country's border with Brazil. The plants, insects and amphibians on these ancient hills of the Guiana shield have evolved from biological ancestors still in Africa. This means that they have developed in total isolation for tens of millions of years since South America drifted away from Africa in the tectonic breakup of the prehistoric land mass known as Gondwanaland.

In 1987-8 I organised and led the Maracá Rainforest Project in an unexplored and uninhabited riverine island at the northern edge of the Amazon rainforests – a beautiful place, with lofty forests, hills and rivers often broken by turbulent rapids. This grew to become the largest research project ever organised in Amazonia by any European country. No less than 150 scientists and a further fifty scientific technicians were involved. We learned much about the dynamics of rainforest ecology. One team studied the hydrological cycle; another group of researchers studied forest regeneration. As well as learning about the geology, soils and ecology of the unexplored marvels of Maracá, the Brazilian environmental agency had also asked us to discover as much as we could about the flora and fauna. Tropical rainforests contain perhaps half the millions of species with which we share this planet, so we could not hope to make a complete inventory of this unknown wilderness. However, the project's botanists, zoologist and entomologists did discover over 200 species of insects and plants that were totally new to science. The biological diversity of the area was astounding, with record numbers of species of spiders, bats, birds and other families of fauna and flora.

To carry out their scientific experiments, the Brazilian and British members of the Maracá Project cut deep into untrodden forests and endured hardships that would have had other adventurers boasting of their exploits – but these explorations were done not for personal glory but in the name of science. Similar expeditions have investigated all the remote parts of the Americas in recent decades. It is such work that makes the present day the golden age of discovery, the time when human beings are learning more than ever before about the natural wonders of our planet. The exploration of the Americas has not yet finished.

A giant of the natural world (*opposite*). In this picture taken by Carleton E. Watkins in California in the 1860s, a man is dwarfed by a *Sequoiadendron giganteum*, or giant sequoia. Individual specimens have been known to reach a girth of 31 metres (101 feet) and a height of 90 metres (300 feet).

Visitors to the Niagara Falls can still stand in the Cave of the Winds, the cavernous space behind the sheet of falling water, as this couple did in the 1860s. Here, however, the experience has become even more extraordinary because the falls have frozen.

274

Mitla, seen here in the 1860s, is one of Mexico's best-known archaeological sites, lying 1480 metres (4855 feet) up in the Sierra Madre del Sur mountains. Mitla means 'place of rest' and is believed orginally to have been a sacred burial ground of the Zapotec people. Around AD 900 Mixtecs began to move down from the north and took over the site from the Zapotecs: it is their architectural influence which is most noticeable in those structures that have survived. The photograph was taken by Désiré Charney, a New Orleans schoolteacher.

The ruins of the Mayan city of Chichén Itzá emerge from the undergrowth. This 1860's photograph by Désiré Charney shows the *monjas*, or nunnery, which dates from the earliest phase of the building. Situated in an arid part of Yucatán, Mexico, the city derived its water – and its name – from two large wells at the site: Chichén Itzá comes from the Mayan words *chi*, or mouths, *chen*, or wells, and *itzá*, the name of the people who settled there. In 1904, the American Edward Herbert Thompson began dredging the Sacred Well – really a small lake – and discovered skeletons and many artefacts. His finds confirmed the legend that sacrificial victims and objects of gold and jade had been thrown into the water to propitiate the rain god believed to live in the depths.

Chicago after the great fire of October 1871. Conditions in the city fuelled the flames: many of Chicago's buildings and its sidewalks were made of wood and there had been no rain for some time. The fire began on 8 October in the southwest and moved to the northeast, even bridging the Chicago River. Lake Michigan, however, proved too formidable a barrier and here the flames died out. Raging for two days, the blaze destroyed an area of 6 square kilometres (2.3 square miles), killing 250 people, making a further 90,000 homeless, and consuming property worth about $200,000,000.

An 1872 expedition party rides along a riverbank in the then relatively uncharted interior of North America *(above)*. The party was engaged in a geological survey of Wyoming set up by the United States Department of the Interior. The photograph was taken by William Henry Jackson, whose work was instrumental in the setting up of Yellowstone National Park in Wyoming.

The Kaieteur Falls on the Potaro River, Guyana (formerly British Guiana), as they were in 1878, in a photograph taken by Sir Everard im Thurn *(opposite)*. Sir Evarard had been sent to British Guiana the previous year to take up a post as curator of the Georgetown Museum. He first visited the falls in 1878 and then again in 1879, being only the second European to set eyes on them. Later, in 1890, he was appointed government agent for British Guiana.

A North American Indian family photographed in Alberta, Canada, in about 1880. The teepee next to which the family sits was perfectly suited to a life on the move. Made from a framework of poles, covered with buffalo skins, and with an opening in the top to act as a chimney, this totally portable dwelling provided both warmth and shelter and gave nomadic or semi-nomadic tribes the mobility they needed to follow the wild herds on which they depended for food.

Two North American Indians, with traditional feathers, beads and tomahawk, pose for the camera of Prince Roland Bonaparte and his *collection anthropologique*, c. 1884. These portraits and others like them, taken barely more than a century ago, reveal the exotic fascination such native peoples had for Europeans of the time. The Bonaparte photographs form an important ethnographic collection.

A group of Ona Indians in Tierra del Fuego, photographed by W. S. Barclay. Tierra del Fuego means 'Land of Fire', and was so named by Ferdinand Magellan after the columns of smoke he saw rising from the land to the south when he first sailed through what is now the Magellan Straits in 1520. Its extreme southerly latitude, however, tipped by the notorious Cape Horn so dreaded by sailors, makes Tierra del Fuego more a land of ice than of fire, as the clothing worn above clearly shows.

An undated photograph by W. S. Barclay. In this lyrically beautiful picture, a small group of Yahgan Indian women and children float serenely across the waters of Tierra del Fuego in a beech-bark canoe. One of the original tribes inhabiting this island wilderness at the southernmost tip of South America, the Yahgan suffered greatly through contact with white newcomers. The greatest agents of their decline were perhaps the Christian missionaries, who unwittingly gave the Yahgan clothing contaminated with diseases against which the Indians had no defence.

Two women from Suriname, formerly Dutch Guiana, on the north coast of South America, wearing traditional dress *(opposite)*. The photograph was taken in 1906. The country's earliest known inhabitants are remembered in its name – they were the Surinen Indians. These women, however, are almost certainly descended from West African slaves brought to Suriname by Dutch colonists to work their flourishing plantations in which sugar, coffee, cacao and other produce were grown.

Tall ships in the harbour of St Lucia, in about 1896 *(above)*. St Lucia is one of the Windward Islands of the West Indies, and its landlocked harbour at Castries was the principal coaling station of the British fleet in the West Indies in the nineteenth century. The island's original inhabitants were Carib Indians, but in 1502, on his fourth voyage to the New World, Christopher Columbus arrived, paving the way for European colonisation.

Two photographs taken for the Bolivia Boundary Commission between 1911 and 1913 *(above)*. It was the Commission's task to decide the boundary between Bolivia and Peru, and this involved considerable field work. The boundary between the two countries was decided on paper in 1912, but it would be another year before demarcation on the ground could be completed. The pictures present two very different views of the same country: the first shows a rustic cantilever bridge spanning Peru's Rio Grande *(above left)*; in contrast, the second *(above right)* shows an arch of weathered rock from the Peru-Bolivia boundary region.

A rider and his dog *(opposite)* in the swamplands of the Paraná River, Argentina, in a memorable picture by W. S. Barclay, who conducted an economic survey of the region in 1908. The Paraná – meaning 'Father of the Waters' in the Guaraní Indian language – is formed by the confluence of the Grande and Paranaíba rivers in southern Brazil. Flowing southward for 4880 kilometres (3032 miles), the lower part of the river crosses a wide flood plain, eventually draining out into the Atlantic near Buenos Aires through a delta 64 kilometres (40 miles) wide at its mouth.

On a 1973 expedition to Roraima, the remote highland state in northern Brazil, this old Akawayo woman *(above)* was photographed by J.C. Wilkins cradling her great-grandchild in a traditional Indian hammock. The Akawayo refer to themselves as 'sky people', because they believe that light, which comes from the heavens and is embodied in the sun, is the source of all life. For this reason, they traditionally bury their dead at dawn, facing the rising sun.

An inhabitant of the Mato Grosso region of central Brazil *(opposite)*. The name of the region comes from the Portuguese for 'dense forest' and this once thickly wooded area provided rare timber, as well as being a source of gold. The photograph was taken in 1928 by George Dyott, an American explorer sent by the Royal Geographical Society to find Colonel Percy Fawcett, lost on an expedition into the Brazilian jungle.

The great American wilderness: a view across the valley to Yosemite Falls in central California *(opposite)*. The falls are divided into two sections, the Upper and Lower Falls, separated by cascades in the middle, forming a total drop of 739 metres (2425 feet). The photograph was taken in about 1917 for the British Official Mission to the United States.

Giant cacti tower above the two figures next to them in this undated Jamaican scene *(above)*. The island's natural vegetation varies from dense bamboo and hardwood forests in the east and northeast – where, in the valleys and foothills, the banana plantations also lie – to dwarf trees and cactus in the dry, savanna-like landscape of the southwest. The island's sugar plantations are situated along the plains of the coastal region.

Two photographs of indigenous Brazilian peoples from the Xingú region of Brazil, taken by the explorer George Dyott. The first *(opposite),* dating from 1931, is of a young female member of either the Kamayurá or Kalapalo tribe, from the Mato Grosso area. The second picture *(above),* taken in 1928, shows a Juruna warrior.

A 1937 photograph taken by the American missionary Miss Martha Moennich, showing a Bororo Indian *(opposite)*. The Bororo, of whom probably fewer than 1000 individuals remain, live mostly north of the Paraguay River in the Mato Grosso, Brazil. The Bororo were famed for their ornamental feather headdresses.

One of the most famous shorelines in the world – that of Rio de Janeiro, captured here in the 1920s *(above)*. The distinctive outline of Sugar Loaf mountain can be seen silhouetted against the water. Paradoxically, there is no river at this location. The name Rio de Janeiro, which means 'river of January', was the one chosen by the Portuguese navigator Gonçalo Coelho who mistook Guanabara Bay for a river mouth on a voyage to the New World in 1501.

Maku Indians listen in on a radio during work for the Bolivia Boundary Commission of 1924-5 *(above)*. Bolivia is bounded by Brazil to the north and east, and this picture was taken in Brazil's Rio Branco region. The Maku follow an ancient way of life, being semi-nomadic forest dwellers who depend for survival largely on their skill as hunters and on what food they can collect in the forest.

A Moennich photograph from 1925 *(opposite)*, almost certainly the last picture of the British explorer Colonel Percy Harrison Fawcett. In the company of his twenty-two-year-old son Jack and Raleigh Rimell, his son's friend, Fawcett set off in search of lost, ancient cities which he believed lay deep in the Xingú rainforest. He failed to return and, although attempts were made to find him, he and his companions were never seen again. Here he is seen riding through typical savanna vegetation towards the headwaters of the Xingú River.

Two Makiritare women with their babies *(above)* examine a camera. The Makiritare Indians, who occupy the southern uplands of the Orinoco River basin, are one of the three main indigenous peoples of the region. The photograph was taken during a 1919-20 expedition to Brazil led by RGS gold medallist Dr. Alexander Hamilton-Rice, who made several expeditions to northwest Amazonia, particularly the upper Rio Negro and Rio Branco regions.

Outside a log cabin in the state of Tennessee, USA, an elderly couple sharpen an axe *(opposite)*. The traditional cabin, the antiquated axe-grinder, and the appearance of the two subjects hint at a way of life unchanged for decades, set against a background of rural poverty. The photograph was taken by G. Barbour in about 1937, during the Great Depression.

A steam locomotive pulling 120 cars loaded with coal runs along the
Pennsylvania Railroad *(above)*. This photograph and the one opposite were
taken in about 1931, for the British Official Mission to the United States.

A famous American landmark: the geyser known as Old Faithful shoots its
column of steam and hot water high into the air *(opposite)*. Old Faithful lies
in Yellowstone Park, the United States' largest nature reserve, set up in
1872 in the Rocky Mountains, Wyoming.

During the Harvard–Dartmouth expedition of 1933-4 to Alaska,
geophysical equipment was set up on the South Brillion glacier *(opposite)*.
Using the principles of physics, such equipment can aid the geological
study of the Earth's surface, interior and atmosphere.

Looking towards Cape Seddon from Melville Bay, Greenland, the view in
winter reveals an endless expanse of ice *(above)*. The bay lies below the
Greenland ice sheet which is second in size only to that of Antarctica. This
photograph, from around 1935, was taken by J. M. Wordie (later president
of the Royal Geographical Society) at the successful completion of the
British Trans-Greenland expedition. The aim of the expedition was to
survey the previously unexplored territory that stretched for 560
kilometres (350 miles) west of Scoresby Sound.

Alaska's Mount McKinley – known as Denali, the 'High One', to local Indians but renamed in 1896 after the then-president of the United States – is North America's highest mountain, reaching an altitude of 6194 metres (20,329 feet). This view, looking up the Huth Glacier, was recorded by Bradford H. Washburn.

San Francisco's famous Golden Gate Bridge rises out of the mist, in
a photograph taken in 1992 by Paul Harris *(opposite)*. The bridge lies
across the Golden Gate, the strait which gives the almost-landlocked
San Francisco Bay access to the Pacific. Erected in 1937, the bridge is
supported by high-tensile steel cables, and has a single span stretching
1280 metres (4200 feet) across the water, making it the second-longest
single-span bridge in the world.

Anchored to a tree trunk by its epiphytic roots, a bromeliad frames the
ruins of a Mayan palace in the Yucatán peninsula, Mexico *(above)*. The
photograph was taken by Michael Freeman in 1993.

A photograph by Eric Lawrie showing the terraced salt beds running down the sides of a gorge near Urubamba, just north of Cuzco in the Peruvian Andes *(opposite)*. A salt worker is visible in the foreground.

Two more photographs by Eric Lawrie, of Bolivian Indians *(above)*. Both wear variations of the distinctive hat – the bowler or trilby – adopted by many South American Indians. The cloth knotted under the woman's chin is known as an *aguayo*, and it is formed into a carrying pouch on the back for holding a baby or to take goods to and from market.

Sunflowers and corn grow in Idaho near the Lost River mountains, close to the site of the world's first nuclear power plant. Just south of the mountains, on the Snake River Plain, lie Atomic City and the US Atomic Energy Commission Reserve. The photograph was taken by Joann Crowther.

A giant salt flat, the Salar de Uyuni, stretches as far as the eye can see in the Andes of southern Bolivia, close to the border with Chile. This *salar*, or salt flat, photographed by Rupert Tenison, is among the larger ones in a chain of salt flats running down through the high Andes from Bolivia into Chile and Argentina.

Climbers on the evocatively named Lost Arrow Spire in Yosemite National Park *(opposite)*, which lies towards the northern end of the Sierra Nevada mountains in California. Yosemite was designated a park in 1890. Such is the outstanding natural beauty and geographic importance of the Sierra that two further conservation areas exist there – the King's Canyon National Park and the Sequoia National Park, lying south of Yosemite. The photograph was taken by Paul Harris.

The peoples of the Andes depend heavily on their herds for their basic needs. Animals such as llamas and sheep provide them with wool for clothing and occasionally with meat, too. In a photograph by Chris Caldicott *(above left)*, a woman leads a llama through the town of Cuzco, Peru. The llama's stamina, surefootedness and ability to go without food for long periods of time make it an ideal beast of burden in this harsh and rugged terrain. Out on the *páramo*, or moorland *(above right)*, a small flock of sheep graze, in a picture by Eric Lawrie. Sheep may be sold for meat to people in the towns.

The Needles in Canyonlands National Park, showing the characteristic red rock of the locality, photographed by Michael Freeman in 1979. Canyonlands lies in eastern Utah, and includes part of the upper course of the Colorado River which cuts its way progressively southward through the rocky plateau and on into the Grand Canyon in Arizona.

One of the most dramatic landmarks in all of North America – Arizona's Grand Canyon *(opposite)*, in a photograph taken by Paul Harris in 1992. The canyon is, in fact, a giant gorge containing the Colorado River. It is 350 kilometres (217 miles) long, 1.5 kilometres (1 mile) deep in parts, and varies from 6 to 29 kilometres (4–18 miles) wide. The Grand Canyon was made a national park in 1919.

A second photograph taken by Paul Harris in the same year *(above)*, showing an aerial view of a gorge in Kokee State Park on the island of Kauai, the northernmost of the eight Hawaiian islands. Although the popular tourist image of these islands is one of palm-fringed beaches, mountains and volcanoes dominate the interiors. The highest peak on Kauai is Kawaikini, at 490 metres (1598 feet).

The futuristic architecture of corporate America – one skyscraper reflected in the glassy façade of another, the Entex building in Houston, Texas *(opposite)*. The photograph was taken in 1978 by Michael Freeman. This style of building was developed in Manhattan in 1868 where land was scarce, and the key component in its construction is a rigid, load-bearing steel frame. The walls, which can be made of relatively flimsy materials such as aluminum or glass, are simply 'hung' from this frame – a technique known as curtain walling.

In contrast to the message of power and wealth conveyed by the picture opposite, these children *(above)* come from the poorest part of Rio de Janeiro – a *favella*, or shanty town. The photographer, Joanna Scadden, had been working with the children in the *favella* and captured this bird's-eye view of them in 1989 while the children were playing organised games.

# selected biographies

Robin Hanbury-Tenison O.B.E.
with Shane Winser

## Isabella L. Bishop née Bird
*(1831 ~ 1904)*

Isabella Bishop was amongst the most indefatigable Victorian lady travellers, leaving behind a legacy of bestsellers that captivated the public. Born on 15 October 1831, the elder daughter of a clergyman, she was a sickly child. At the age of twenty-six Isabella was prescribed a sea voyage. She sailed to Halifax, Nova Scotia and returned seven months later having travelled widely in the eastern United States and Canada. Her first book, *The Englishwoman in America,* was based on her letters home. She returned to America the following year, travelling from the Deep South to the Hudson Bay, meeting Longfellow, Emerson and Thoreau, and witnessing the American religious revival of the time.

In 1872 she set off for Hawaii, at that time called the Sandwich Islands, then moved on to Colorado where she met heavy-drinking Rocky Mountain Jim Nugent with whom she climbed Long's Peak in Estes Park. Their relationship is described in her bestselling *A Lady's Life in the Rocky Mountains* (1879). An ardent social reformer, Isabella helped raise funds for the Medical Missionary School in Edinburgh before travelling to Japan where, with her servant Ito, she travelled 1130 kilometres (700 miles) and visited the 'hairy' Ainus on Hokkaido island. Her return journey via Singapore and the Malay states was described in *The Golden Chersonese and the Way Thither* (1883).

After the death of her husband John Bishop, Isabella devoted herself to establishing medical missions, and trained as a nurse, before setting off for Tibet with two servants and an Afghan soldier, Usman Shan, to escort her. An invitation to join a survey expedition followed which led her 4000 kilometres (2500 miles) though Persia, Kurdistan and Armenia on one of the toughest journeys of her career. In 1892, Isabella was amongst the first fifteen women to be elected to Fellowship of the Royal Geographical Society.

Isabella took up the study of photography, and in 1894 set off on the first of her four visits to Korea. She took a steam boat up the Yangtze River in 1896 and, accompanied by her servant Paoning Fu, travelled overland to Szechwan, finally arriving back in Shanghai after a journey of 12,875 kilometres (8000 miles). She made one final journey, on horseback, to the Atlas Mountains in 1901.

## Prince Roland-Napoleon Bonaparte
*(1858 ~ 1924)*

Prince Roland-Napoleon Bonaparte, scholar, soldier, scientist, photographer, and generous benefactor to the Academie des Sciences, dedicated his life to the promotion of science in France. Born in Paris on 19 May 1858, he was the grandson of Lucien Bonaparte, estranged brother to the Emperor. In 1877 Roland-Napoleon was enrolled at the Saint-Cyr Military Academy, graduating two years later at the top of his class. He was forced to abandon his military career at the age of twenty-eight, however, when the Republican government banned members of the French aristocracy from military service. His

Isabella L Bird, *page 37*

Prince Bonaparte, *page 283*

Douglas Carruthers, *pages 50, 51, 58, 59, 66*

wife died in childbirth, and Roland-Napoleon dedicated himself to his daughter's upbringing and to his scientific studies. He assembled a magnificent scientific, historical and geographical library, celebrated throughout France, the core of which remains an important part of the national heritage to this day.

In 1884 he published his first great anthropological work, *The People of Surinam,* inspired by notes taken during the colonial exhibition in Amsterdam in 1883. This kindled a passionate interest in other indigenous peoples. Roland undertook several trips to Germany, Italy and Corsica in order to verify details of the Napoleonic Wars, and published his findings in 1891. He also sought to examine all aspects of contemporary life in Europe and North America. During the same period he conducted and published studies of glaciers in Switzerland and the French Alps, establishing observation stations throughout the area; supported the 1901-2 expedition by Colonel Bourgeois to measure the meridian of the Equator; funded the Banyul-Roscoff zoological laboratories; and helped establish the Mont Blanc observatory. He also assembled a herbarium of more than 300,000 species of plants.

In 1907 Roland was appointed to sit as a free member of the Academie des Sciences, and in 1919, in recognition of a life dedicated to the promotion of sciences, he was elected President of the prestigious Société de Geographie. Three years later he was appointed President of the International Geographic Union in Brussels. During his illustrious career, he also held office as President of the French Glacier Society and the French Speleological Society.

# Douglas Carruthers
## *(1882 ~ 1962)*

Douglas Carruthers, explorer, zoologist and cartographer, was born on 4 October 1882. As a boy he wrote that he wanted to go to what was then called 'Darkest Africa', to see the rock-hewn ruins of Petra, and to reach 'that strange capital at the back of the world, Bukhara': he had done all three by the age of twenty-six. He studied at Cambridge University, but left early as he was attracted to the practical aspects of zoological collecting, and was apprenticed to the leading taxidermist at the Natural History Museum in London. In 1904-5 whilst with the American University at Beirut he made collections, particularly of birds, that were sent back to England. This led to an invitation to join the 1905-6 British Museum Ruwenzori Mountains expedition with Wollaston, with whom he subsequently crossed Africa from east to west, down the Congo river.

In 1907-8 Carruthers spent two years in what was then Russian Turkestan exploring the Tienshan mountains and making scientific collections with Mr Rickmers, a Hamburg shipowner, in an area virtually unvisited by Westerners. He then went in search of the rare White Oryx in the Central Arabian desert, an experience described in *Arabian Adventure* (1935). His most remarkable journey, however, took place in 1910-11 when, with J. H. Miller, a big-game hunter, and M. P. Price, he crossed Central Asia from Central Siberia to the headwaters of the Yenesei into Outer Mongolia, and across the Altai into the Gobi Desert by horse and camel. For this achievement, recorded in

Desiré Charnay, *pages 276, 277*

Ernest Gedge, *page 110*

the two-volume *Unknown Mongolia* (1913), he received the Patron's Gold Medal of the Royal Geographical Society. A reconnaissance expedition into Anatolia and Turkish Asia Minor followed. During World War I he worked on maps for the Allied campaign against the Turks, based on data supplied by T. E. Lawrence, Captain Shakespear, Gertrude Bell and Philby.

## Desiré Charnay
*(1828 ~ 1915)*

Claude-Joseph Desiré Charnay was born in the Rhone district of France, studied at the Lycée Charlemagne in Paris and settled in New Orleans in 1850 where he worked as a schoolteacher. Keen to travel, he toured the United States, and gained the support of the French Ministry of Public Instruction for a visit to the Yucatán. He arrived in Mexico in the midst of the Civil War, and spent ten months in Mexico City before finally reaching Yucatán, where he photographed pre-Columbian ruins. He returned to France in 1861 and published a portfolio of forty-nine views titled *Cites et Ruines Americaines, Mitla, Palenque, Izamal, Chichen-Itza, Uxmal*. Charnay was the official photographer to the French expedition to Madagascar in 1863, before returning to Mexico the following year. He left Mexico at the collapse of the Maximillian government in 1867, and was commissioned by the magazine *Le Tour de Monde* to visit Brazil, Chile and Argentina, and by the French government to go to Java and Australia. From 1880-2 Charnay excavated and photographed ruins in Yucatán resulting in *Les Anciennes Villes du*

*Nouveau Monde* (1885) and many other books and articles. In 1897 he visited Yemen, before retiring to Paris where he wrote popular travelogues and novels based on his journeys.

## Ernest Gedge
*(1862 ~ 1935)*

Ernest Gedge was an amateur photographer of considerable merit. At the age of seventeen, he went to Assam as a tea planter and then joined the Imperial British East Africa Company. In 1889 he and F. J. (later Sir Frederick) Jackson set off on an expedition into the interior, reaching Buganda in April 1890, where Gedge remained to represent the Company. Before his departure to London in January 1891, he travelled into German territory to the southwest of Lake Victoria. Back in London, he assisted Macdonald in his preparations for the Uganda Railway Survey, and later returned to East Africa as special correspondent for *The Times*. His photographs illustrate Sir Frederick Jackson's *Early Days in East Africa* (1930), compiled by Lady Jackson after her husband's death in 1929. A fine collection is also held in the Secretariat library, Entebbe.

## Francis Frith
*(1822 ~ 1898)*

Francis Frith was one of the leading British topographical photographers and publishers of the nineteenth century. Born into a Quaker family from Chesterfield, he started work in a

Francis Frith, *page 35*

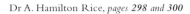

Dr A. Hamilton Rice, *pages 298 and 300*

wholesale grocers in Liverpool, but was quickly bored. Between 1856 and 1859 he undertook a series of expeditions to Egypt, Nubia, Palestine and Syria to photograph the classical sites which had fascinated travellers for centuries. He carefully documented all the monuments listed in Sir Gardner Wilkinson's *Handbook for Travellers in Egypt*, amongst them the pyramids, the Sphinx, Abu Simbel and the Great Temple at Philae, to produce images he knew would be popular with his customers back in Britain. To ease his passage he dressed as a Turk, using a turban to hide his European hair. His darkroom wagon was thought to contain his harem. Although Frith used a variety of different-sized cameras, he often used unusually large format glass-plate negatives, which were difficult to prepare and process in the heat but produced outstanding results. Frith's detailed images are now of considerable historical importance because many of the archaeological sites he visited have now been transformed, either by the flooding needed to create the second Aswan Dam or because they have been vandalised. They were also an outstanding commercial success. Two thousand copies of his lavish book *Egypt and Palestine Photographed and Described* were published. A successful career followed.

In 1860 Frith and Co. was established in Reigate, from where photographers were sent off around the world. Over the next ten years Frith became the largest manufacturer of photographs, particularly postcards and photographic accessories such as leather albums and frames. Frith married and continued to travel but worked closer to home, in Britain and on the Continent. Frith and Co. stayed in business for over a century.

# Dr A. Hamilton Rice
## (1875 ~ 1956)

Hamilton Rice was amongst the greatest of the twentieth-century explorers of South America. Born in Boston in 1875, he was educated at Harvard and went on to study medicine, qualifying in 1904, by which time he had already begun his career as an explorer. He travelled to Spitsbergen, Russia and the Caucasus in 1897, the west coast of the Hudson Bay in 1899, and two years later followed Orellana's journey down the Amazon. He came to London to learn the survey techniques required to map quickly and accurately in remote regions, and in 1910 took the RGS's Survey Diploma. During World War I he was a surgeon attached to the American Hospital at Neuilly, but was later commissioned into the Navy and eventually became director of the navigation school at Newport, Rhode Island.

Dr Rice's area of exploration was the northwestern Amazon basin and, from 1907 onwards, he examined and mapped the region's hitherto little-known rivers. He investigated the Casiquaire Canal, the natural waterway linking the Orinoco and Amazon Rivers, and carried out research into the natural history and medical geography of the region. His last expedition in 1924-5 was to the easterly tributaries of the Rio Negro. For this he used a hydroplane for reconnaissance, and was the first to make use of shortwave wireless in the field. He regularly used air photography for geographical exploration. He had a close affiliation with Britain and was a Gold Medallist, Vice President and generous benefactor of the Royal Geographical Society.

Charles Howard-Bury, *page 23*

Frank Hurley, *pages 169, 170,* **171r***, 176, 178, 179r, 180,* **182***, 183*

# Charles Howard-Bury
## *(1883 ~ 1963)*

Leader of the first expedition to Mount Everest in 1921, Charles Kenneth Howard-Bury was born on 15 August 1883, educated at Eton and Sandhurst, and joined the 60th Rifles. Before World War I he learnt to climb in the Tyrol, and when stationed in India spent his leaves on shooting forays in the Tien Shan and in Russian and Chinese Turkestan. In 1905, he entered Tibet illegally through Kumoan, and in 1909 visited Kashmir and the Karakoram. After the war, during which he was awarded the DSO, he became Parliamentary Private Secretary to the Secretary of State for War (1922-4).

On behalf of the Joint Himalayan Committee of the Alpine Club and the Royal Geographical Society, Howard made two visits to India in 1919 and 1920 to get permission for an attempt on Mount Everest. The Dalai Lama finally gave his blessing to an approach through Tibet early in 1921, and Howard-Bury was invited to lead the expedition. Despite the death of Dr Kellas, the most experienced high-altitude climber, the expedition made a thorough exploration of the approach, and Mallory and Bullock's ascent to the North Col laid the foundations for all future attempts to climb Everest until World War II. Howard-Bury himself reached 8000 metres (22,000 feet) on the Lapka La. After retiring from Parliament in 1931, he lived in Ireland with intervals of travel and big game hunting. He also bred racehorses, one of which called Everest was born in 1953 within days of the peak's ascent, and won him several races.

# Frank Hurley
## *(1890 ~ 1962)*

An Australian photographer and explorer, Frank Hurley began his career with a firm of photographers, but soon left to join Douglas Mawson on his Australian Antarctic Expedition of 1911-14, during which he was one of the party that sledged to the South Magnetic Pole. On his return, he joined Shackleton's Imperial Trans-Antarctic Expedition of 1914-17, and brought back memorable photographs of the wreck of the *Endurance* and scenes of Elephant Island. He also made a documentary film, *In the Grip of the Polar Ice*. Ten days after the rescued party returned to London, Hurley became official war photographer in France and served there and in the Middle East for the rest of World War I. Filming ventures in New Guinea and Central Australia and lecture tours in America followed. In 1929-31 he joined the British, Australian, New Zealand Antarctic Research Expedition, and in 1939 he again became a war photographer. Among his publications are *Pearls and Savages* (Sydney, 1924), *Argonauts of the South* (London, 1927), *Shackleton's Argonauts* (London, 1948) and *Glorious Queensland* (Sydney, 1950).

# Sir Harry Johnston
## *(1858 ~ 1927)*

Henry Hamilton Johnston, colonial administrator and explorer of Africa, was born at Kennington on 12 June 1858, educated at Stockwell Grammar School and King's College, London, before

Sir Harry Johnston, *pages 120, 121, 122, 125*

Frank Kingdon-Ward,
*pages 64, 67, 68, 69*

Mrs Patrick Ness, *page 248*

spending four years studying art at the Royal Academy where he became an accomplished watercolourist. He had an early aptitude for natural history and languages, and a visit to Tunisia at the age of twenty-one generated a lifelong interest in Africa.

In 1882 Johnston accompanied Lord Mayo to Southern Angola, and then went on alone to the Congo. In 1884 he led a joint British Association and Royal Society scientific expedition to Mount Kilimanjaro. The *Daily Telegraph* commissioned him to act as its correspondent, and whilst in East Africa Johnston negotiated treaties with the chiefs of Moshi and Taveta that helped lay the foundation of British East Africa. In 1885 he was appointed Vice-Consul for the Cameroons and the Niger Delta, and during the three years he spent in the Gulf of Guinea he helped set up the British administration in the Delta and climbed Mount Cameroon, making natural history collections for the British Museum. He was then sent as Consul to Portuguese East Africa and, by the time he left in 1897, had formed treaties which brought not only the Nyasaland protectorate but also much of Northern Rhodesia under British control. He spent two years as Consul-General in Tunis, before taking up his last official appointment as Special Commissioner to Uganda in 1899-1901, during which he explored part of the Ruwenzori range and the Semliki Forest, where he obtained the first entire skin of an Okapi, that rare and reclusive forest animal.

After his retirement he took a special interest in Liberia, and concentrated on his seminal two-volume work on the Bantu languages. He published more than forty books on the geography of Africa.

# Frank Kingdon-Ward
## *(1885 ~ 1958)*

Frank Kingdon-Ward was born in 1885, the son of a Professor of Botany at Cambridge University, where he also studied before taking up a teaching post in Shanghai. In 1906 he went on what was to be the first of a series of plant-hunting expeditions over the next fifty years into the vast complex of mountains where China, Tibet, India and Burma meet. Specialising in rhododendrons, primulas, lilies, gentians and poppies, his introductions immeasurably enriched English gardens. For the last ten years of his life he was accompanied on his travels by his second wife, Jean Macklin; these included a nightmare journey through the earthquake-shattered Mishmi Hills. He was an outstanding travel writer and scientist, and a Gold Medallist of the Royal Geographical Society.

# Mrs Patrick Ness
## *(c. 1880 ~ 1962)*

Elizabeth Wilhelmina Ness, widow of Major Patrick Ness, was the first woman to become a Council member of the Royal Geographical Society. In 1953 she endowed the Mrs Patrick Ness Award to be presented by the RGS 'either to travellers who have successfully carried out their plans, or to encourage travellers who wish to pursue or follow-up investigations which have been partially completed'. Mrs Ness's own travels included a journey to Victoria Nyaza in 1906 and elsewhere in Central

John (Jack) Noel, *pages 11, 63, 70*

Harry St John Philby, *page 202*

Africa, including the Mount Kenya region in 1908-9, 1911-12 and 1913. In 1923 she travelled from Beirut across the Syrian desert to Isfahan in Persia. Her travels are described in *Ten Thousand Miles in Two Continents*, published in 1929. A competent photographer, she was one of the first travellers to use 16mm cinematographic film in colour.

## John (Jack) Noel
### (1890 ~ 1989)

Photographer and filmmaker John Baptist Lucius Noel was born at Newton Abbott, Devon into a military family. He was schooled in Lausanne where he learnt to ski and climb and then studied painting in Florence before joining the British Army in northern India. He spent his leave exploring the Sikkim-Tibetan border attempting to find a route to Everest at a time when both Tibet and Nepal were firmly closed to foreigners. In 1913, travelling in disguise, he got to within sixty-four kilometres (forty miles) of the mountain before being arrested. During World War I he served on the Western Front, was captured by the Germans but escaped under cover of darkness. In World War II he worked for the intelligence service for four years.

In 1919 Sir Francis Younghusband invited Noel to lecture to members of the Royal Geographical Society and the Alpine Club on the subject of his book *Through Tibet to Everest*, to help promote a British reconnaissance expedition to Everest. Although Noel was unable to join the 1921 expedition, he resigned his commission to be a member of the 1922 Everest

expedition led by General Bruce. Noel set up a specially designed darkroom at base camp to process some 5500 metres (18,000 feet) of film which was washed in river water pumped up by Sherpas, and dried over a yak-dung fire. He had a special lightweight camera designed to withstand the cold, and spent a fortnight at 7010 metres (23,000 feet) on the North Col, a record height for photography at that time.

In 1924, convinced that Everest would be climbed this time, Noel offered £8000 to the Everest Committee for the full photographic rights to the expedition. A laboratory was built in Darjeeling to process the film sent down from the mountain by teams of riders on ponies. When climbers Mallory and Irvine went missing 700 metres (2300 feet) from the summit, Noel's hopes of financial success were ruined. Instead of a film of the first ascent of the world's highest mountain, all he was left with was a travelogue of an expedition into Tibet. A live performance by visiting Tibetan lamas accompanied showings in Britain but angered the Dalai Lama, and put a stop to any future expeditions to Everest for almost a decade. Copies of Noel's 1922 and 1924 films are now held by the National Film Archive and are still regularly used in documentaries about Everest.

## Harry St John Philby
### (1885 ~ 1960)

Arabist and explorer, Harry St John Bridger Philby was born in Ceylon where his father was a tea planter. He studied Arabic, Urdu and Hindi at Trinity College, Cambridge, and joined the

Herbert Ponting, *pages 18, 46, 48, 172, 173, 174, 177, 179r*

Indian Civil Service in 1908. At the beginning of World War I Philby was sent to Baghdad as a political officer, and in 1917 to Riyadh to negotiate with Ibn Saud. He used this opportunity to visit the interior, crossing the Arabian Peninsula by camel from Qatar to Jidda, the first European to do so for nearly a century.

In 1918 Philby explored the Nejd, a large area of south-central Arabia, which he wrote about in *The Heart of Arabia* (1923), and was awarded the Founder's Medal of the Royal Geographical Society in 1920. He went on to explore the Syrian desert between Amman in Jordan and the upper Euphrates, but retired from government service in 1924 after quarrelling with the British government over its policy in Arabia. He converted to Islam and continued to live in Arabia where he had a number of business interests.

In 1932 Philby made his epic crossing of the Empty Quarter or *Rub' al Khali* in search of the 'lost city' of Wabar, and found meteorite fragments which some Muslim authorities considered might substantiate biblical stories of the city's destruction. Although Bertram Thomas is credited with the first crossing of the Empty Quarter in 1931, many believe Philby's journey a year later was more arduous. Philby went on to explore the Hadramaut, described in *Sheba's Daughters* (1939). His collections of plants, animals and fossils, deposited in museums in Britain and North America, made a major contribution to the understanding of the natural history of Arabia. When oil was discovered in Saudi Arabia, Philby was amongst Ibn Saud's key advisors and guided him and his ministers through the massive changes that ensued.

# Herbert Ponting
## *(1870 ~ 1935)*

Born in Salisbury, Herbert George Ponting ranched and mined in California before becoming a professional photographer in 1900. As correspondent for *Harper's Weekly* in the Russo-Japanese War, he travelled widely in the Far East, visiting India, China, Korea, Java and Burma. Japan had a particularly profound effect on him and he published *In Lotus-land Japan* (London, 1910) before he joined the British Antarctic expedition of 1910-13 – Scott's tragic, last expedition – as official photographer, or 'camera artist' as he preferred to be called. Under the leadership of Captain Robert Falcon Scott, the object of the expedition was mainly scientific although an attempt to reach the South Pole was also planned. Ponting joined the expedition in New Zealand and sailed South on the *Terra Nova* which nearly sank in high seas off Campbell Island. He spent fourteen months based at the hut at Cape Evans, photographing the beauty of the Antarctic landscape and its wildlife and documenting the activities of the expedition, which was not always popular because it involved posing in all sorts of uncomfortable positions until nearly frozen.

Ponting's technical and artistic skills resulted in outstanding black and white and early Autochrome colour photographs, as well as some of the first movie film, recording the events leading up to one of the great tragedies in the history of exploration. He filmed Scott and his party depart for the pole from the foot of the Great Ice Barrier, with the memorable

Captain W.H.I. Shakespear, *pages 196, 199, 200, 201, 212*

Sir (Marc) Aurel Stein

image of Bill Wilson turning to wave farewell. Ponting left the expedition with the relief ship in 1912, his job done. Although his film of the expedition *Ninety Degrees South* was shown many times and remade in 1933, and a second book *The Great White South* was published in 1921, Ponting's various commercial ventures were never entirely successful.

## Captain W. H. I. Shakespear
*(1878 ~ 1915)*

One of the most significant explorers of eastern and central Arabia, William Henry I. Shakespear was born in India in 1878, the son of a colonial officer in the Indian Forest Service. He served with the Bengal Lancers before transferring to the consular service and was posted to Persia and eastern Arabia, later becoming political agent in Kuwait. A pioneer motorist, in 1907 he drove his single-cylinder Rover to and from England and the Persian Gulf, and then in 1912 from Bombay to Delhi. He made six exploratory journeys in eastern Arabia, and in 1914 crossed the Arabian Peninsula from Kuwait via Riyadh to Sinai, travelling across nearly 2000 kilometres (1230 miles) of unknown country.

　　As political agent in Kuwait, Shakespear became convinced that Ibn Saud was the only Arab leader capable of bringing together the disparate tribes of the desert in an alliance with Britain against the Turks in the case of war. Despite a series of detailed reports which he sent back home, he was unable to convince the Foreign Office of his view. When war did break

out, Shakespear was called on to negotiate. On 24 January 1915, however, at the age of thirty-six, he was tragically killed fighting alongside Ibn Saud against his pro-Turkish enemy, Ibn Rashid bin Hail. In time, Shakespear's predictions turned out to be correct. Ibn Saud became one of the most powerful rulers in the world, and the British had needlessly put themselves at a disadvantage with the Arabs for years to come.

## Sir (Marc) Aurel Stein
*(1862 ~ 1943)*

Sir (Marc) Aurel Stein, explorer and archaeologist, was born in Budapest, emigrated to England, and worked on early coins at the British Museum before becoming Principal of the Oriental College in Lahore. Inspired by Sven Hedin, he carried out a reconnaissance of the Taklamakan desert in 1897 which led to five major expeditions in Chinese Turkestan between 1907 and 1929. During these, Stein discovered important relics of the trade along the once-flourishing silk routes from Rome to China, and excavated buried cities which showed that Central Asia had once been a fertile plain. He discovered the Cave of the Thousand Buddhas near Tan Huang containing ancient scrolls of which 9000 were removed and are now in the British Museum. This was perhaps the greatest find of early Buddhist manuscripts and Stein has been criticised for removing them. However, many of those left behind have since been stolen or destroyed. He was superintendent of the Indian Archaeological Survey 1910-29. He is buried in the Christian cemetery at Kabul.

Wilfred Thesiger, *pages 216, 217, 218*

John Thomson, *pages 32, 39, 49*

# Sir Wilfred Thesiger
*(born 1910)*

Wilfred Patrick Thesiger was born in Addis Ababa and educated at Eton and Magdalen College, Oxford. He returned to Ethiopia to attend the coronation of Haile Selassie in 1930, and went on to hunt and travel with the Danakil tribes. He joined the Sudan political service in 1935, and whilst on leave travelled across the Sahara to the Tibesti Mountains. During World War II he served in Ethiopia, Syria and with the SAS in the Western desert. After the war he travelled with the Bedu in the Empty Quarter of southern Arabia and Oman which he described in *Arabian Sands* (1959), and lived with the Marsh Arabs of Iraq for nearly seven years. His travels elsewhere have included the Zagros mountains in Iran, the Hindu Kush and Karakoram Mountains, Nuristan, and the South China Sea. From the early 1960s he made his home in northern Kenya. His biography, *The Life of My Choice*, and *Visions of a Nomad,* a selection of his favourite photographs taken with a Leica camera and protected from sand, frost or the miasma of the marshes in a little goat-skin bag, were both published in 1987.

# John Thomson
*(1837 ~ 1921)*

Pioneer photojournalist and travel photographer, John Thomson was born in Edinburgh in 1837 and studied chemistry at university there. Before settling down to a career as a professional photographer in London, he decided to travel in Asia to use photography to record the characteristic features of the countries and peoples of the Far East. He set out on an overland journey for Ceylon (Sri Lanka) in 1862 but became ill and had to return home. He set out again in 1865 for the Malay Peninsula, and after working there for some time, went on to Thailand and Cambodia where some of his best photographs were taken. He recorded the famous Angkor Wat ruins, later publishing the photographs in the two-volume *Antiquities of Cambodia* (1867). Leaving Cambodia, he proceeded to Macao and Hong Kong, and then on to Formosa. In China, he visited Shanghai and travelled 2000 kilometres (3200 miles) up the Yagtze from Nanking through the gorges to the mountains of Szechuan, and on to Peking. The results of his travels were published in 1873 in four handsome folio volumes containing an extensive collection of high-quality photographs of landscapes, cities, buildings and people, with accompanying text. In 1875 he published a general narrative of his travels, *The Straits of Malacca, Indo-China, and China: Ten Years' Travels, Adventures, and Residence in the Far East*. In 1877 Thomson worked with sociologist Adolphe Smith to produce a series of photographs and articles on the seamier side of London's steet life. When Britain took over Cyprus in 1878, Thomson visited the island with his camera and published the results in two illustrated quarto volumes. From 1886 Thompson was Instructor of Photography for the Royal Geographical Society, where he was able to tutor many of the explorers of the time while promoting photography as a documentary tool. Henry Stanley was amongst his pupils.

Bradford Washburn, *page 308*

Carleton E. Watkins *pages 266, 273, 303*

# Bradford Washburn
## *(born 1910)*

Henry Bradford Washburn Jr, mountaineer, photographer and cartographer, was born in Boston, USA and spent his summers climbing and hiking with his family both in North America and the European Alps where he developed his outstanding talents as a photographer and filmmaker. With the proceeds of his lectures and films, he managed to part-finance his studies at Harvard in French history and literature, and later surveying and aerial photography. Newly qualified as a pilot, he joined the staff at Harvard's University Institute of Geographical Exploration, and led the Harvard-Dartmouth Alaskan expeditions to map Mount Crillon. He was subsequently invited to lead the 1935 National Geographic Yukon expedition which mapped 8050 kilometres (5000 miles) of the St Elias Range from the air and on the ground using skis and dog teams in mid-winter. His photographs and the accompanying story about his ascent of Mount Lucania, in the same range, at that time the highest unclimbed mountain in North America, appeared in *Life* magazine in 1937.

      Soon after, he became Director of the Boston Museum of Natural History (now the Boston Museum of Science) and set about its modernisation. He married Barbara Polk, and on their honeymoon, they made the first ascent of Mount Bertha in Alaska. She became the first woman to climb Mount McKinley in 1947. With the support of the Museum and the *National Geographic,* Washburn continued his surveys of Mount McKinley, the Grand Canyon (*National Geographic,* July 1978), and Mount

Washington and the Presidentials in his native New England. In 1988 he completed a life-long ambition to map Mount Everest from the air at a scale of 1:50,000 – a feat which involved eleven different nations, a Learjet to take aerial photographs of 1130 square kilometres (700 square miles) of the Everest region in cloudless conditions, and a team of Swiss mapmakers two years to translate these images onto paper.

# Carleton E. Watkins
## *(1829 ~ 1916)*

Carleton E. Watkins was one of the great pioneers of American landscape photography. In the 1840s he left New York and headed west to make his fortune in the Calfornia Gold Rush, but ended up working in Robert Vance's photographic studio in San José. In 1861 he made his first trip to Yosemite Valley, using mules and a wagon to transport his equipment.

      Watkins opened the Yosemite Art Gallery in San Francisco to exhibit and sell framed prints of the resulting photographs, which were taken on 15 x 20-inch glass plates. These images and others taken on subsequent expeditions throughout California were later exhibited at the Paris Universal Exhibition of 1867 and Watkins' fame spread to Europe. Unfortunately his eyesight deteriorated, and the 1906 San Francisco earthquake and fire destroyed much of his work. Those albums and prints which survived were re-discovered after the end of World War II, and are now highly prized pieces of photographic work.

# about the authors

## Christina Dodwell
Ms Dodwell is an RGS Fellow and recipient of the Royal Scottish Geographical Society's Mungo Park Medal (1989). She is the author of nine books, and has made many documentaries. She is founder of The Dodwell Trust, a Third World charity.

## Sir Ranulph T-W-Fiennes Bt
Sir Ranulph Twistleton-Wykeham-Fiennes has led six major British expeditions, notably the Transglobe (1979-82), the first surface journey around the world's polar axis, and the South Polar Unsupported Expedition (1992-93), the longest polar journey in history. His publications include *To the Ends of the Earth* (1983) and *Living Dangerously* (1995).

## Michael Freeman
A prolific photographer and writer, Michael Freeman launched his career with a trip down the Amazon in 1971. Photos of his travels have been appearing ever since, recent commissions including *Ancient Capitals of Thailand* (1995) and *Palaces of Bangkok* (1996). He is the author of 23 books on photography.

## Robin Hanbury-Tenison OBE
RGS Gold Medallist and long-time RGS Council member, Robin Hanbury-Tenison led the RGS Mulu Expedition in 1977-78, and has participated in many more. He is President of Survival International, which campaigns for the rights of indigenous peoples, and is the author of *A Question of Survival* (1970) and *Mulu: the Rain Forest* (1980), among others.

## Dr. John Hemming
Dr Hemming was Director and Secretary of the RGS from 1975 to 1996. He promoted twelve major RGS research projects, and personally led the largest, the Maracá Rainforest Project in Brazil. He has been on numerous expeditions, particularly to unexplored parts of Amazonia.

## Sir Edmund Hillary
Mountaineer, author and RGS Gold Medallist Sir Edmund Hillary was knighted for scaling the summit of Mount Everest with Sherpa Tenzing in 1953. He served as New Zealand's High Commissioner to India, Nepal and Bangladesh (1985-88), and has been active in fostering development and humanitarian projects in these areas.

## The Rt. Hon. the Earl Jellicoe
Lord Jellicoe has led a distinguished political, diplomatic and business career, and holds the Legion d'Honneur, Croix de Guerre, Greek Order of Honour and Greek War Cross. He became President of the RGS in 1993.

## Dr. Richard Leakey
Dr Leakey is a distinguished anthropologist and conservationist. He is Chairman of the Wildlife Clubs of Kenya Association and the Foundation for Research into Origin of Man. He presented the BBC TV series *The Making of Mankind* (1981), and wrote the accompanying book. His other publications include *People of the Lake* (1979) and *One Life* (1984).

# acknowledgments

## photographs

Copyright notice: All efforts have been made to contact the copyright owners of photographs where rights have not previously been assigned by the Royal Geographical Society, as indicated below.

FRONT COVER John Evans  BACK COVER Frank Hurley

### ASIA
(Opening photograph: View of Lake Yamanaka from the summit of Mt. Fuji, Japan, taken by Herbert Ponting in 1907)
Herbert Ponting 18, 46, 47, 48. Paul Harris 72l, 73, 77, 81, 82, 84, 85. Maurice Joseph 72r. Edmund Hillary 74. George Bard 75. Steve Razzetti 76. Paul Harris 77, 81, 82, 84, 85. Ian Cumming 78, 79, 80. Chris Caldicott 83, 86r, 87, 88, 89. David Constantine 86l, 92l, 93. Michael Freeman 90, 91. Norma Joseph 92r.

### AFRICA
(Opening photograph: Sahara caravan in the 1880s, Algeria, Anon)
Michael Freeman 140, 141, 149. Adrian Arbib 142, 143, 147r. Sir Peter Holmes 144, 155. John Evans 145, 151r. Chris Caldicott 146, 148, 154. Chris Bradley 147l. John R. Jones 150, 158, 159. John Miles 151l, 152, 153. Norma Joseph 156. Maurice Joseph 157.

### THE POLES
(Opening photograph: Shackleton's ship Endurance caught in the ice, taken by Frank Hurley in 1915)
Herbert Ponting 172, 173, 174, 177, 179. Colonel Andrew Croft 184. US Navy for US Geological Survey 185. Charles Swithinbank 186, 187, 189. Bruce Herrod 188. Sir Ranulph Fiennes 190. Stephen Venables 191. Martha Holmes 192, 194. Drew Geldart 193. Roger Mear 195.

### THE MIDDLE EAST
(Opening photograph: Ibn Saud's army on the march in 1911, taken by Captain W.H.I. Shakespear)
E.B. Schochsack 213. Sir Wilfred Thesiger 216, 217, 218. Sir Peter Holmes 220, 221. Chris Caldicott 222, 224l, 227. Paul Harris 223. Patrick Syder 224r, 226. Dr Stephen Coyne 225. Nigel Winser 228. Chris Bradley 229. Unknown 235.

### AUSTRALASIA
(Opening photograph: A beach in Papua New Guinea, taken by R.E. Guise, 1898)
Unknown 251. Michael Leahy 254, 271. Edward Mendell 256, 261, 263r. Adrian Arbib 257l. Paul Harris 257r, 262. Joann Crowther 258, 259, 260r, 264. John Miles 260l, 263l. Chris Wright 265.

### AMERICAS
(Opening photograph: The Central Pacific Railroad in Yosemite Valley, California, taken by Carleton E. Watkins c.1860)
J.C. Wilkins 290. National Geographic Society 301. British Official Mission to the United States 302, 304. Bradford H. Washburn 309. Paul Harris 310, 316, 320, 321. Michael Freeman 311, 318, 319, 322. Eric Lawrie 312, 313, 317l. Joann Crowther 314. Rupert Tenison 315. Chris Caldicott 317. Joanna Scadden 323.

Colour Separation: Bright Arts Graphics (S) Pte Ltd

## bibliography

The essay on page 162 by Sir Ranulph Fiennes contains extracts from the following works: *The Great Antarctic Rescue* by F.A. Worsley (Times Books), *Across the Top of the World* by Wally Herbert (Longmans) with kind permission of Wally Herbert, *The Crossing of Antarctica* by Sir Vivian Fuchs, Sir Edmund Hillary (Simon & Schuster, US), *The Worst Journey in the World* by Apsley Cherry-Garrard (Macmillan) with thanks to Mrs Apsley Cherry-Garrard, *Mawson's Will* by Lennard Bickel (Avon Books), *Shackleton* by Roland Huntford (Abacus, Little, Brown) with kind permission of A.P. Watt on behalf of Roland Huntford, *Scott of the Antarctic* by Elspeth Huxley (Weidenfeld & Nicholson) with kind permission of the estate of Elspeth Huxley.

Sir Wilfred Thesiger's essay on page 198 is an extract from *Desert, Marsh and Mountain: The World of a Nomad* (Collins 1979). Copyright © Wilfred Thesiger 1979. Facilitated by Curtis Brown on behalf of Wilfred Thesiger.

The publishers have attempted to contact the copyright owners of the literary works from which extracts have been taken in this book. The publisher apologises if inadvertently permission has not been obtained from a copyright owner to include any extract from a copyright work.

## with thanks

The publishers would like to extend their thanks to all those that have contributed to the making of the book, in particular the following:
All at the Royal Geographical Society, especially Joanna Scadden and Daisy Jellicoe of the Society's photographic library; Janet Turner, Shelagh Nott and Rachel Rowe of the Society's book library; Dr Rita Gardner, Nigel Winser, Shane Winser and Dr Andrew Tatham; and the explorers and photographers, their families and friends, who have contributed to the Society's archives over the years. Also thanks to John North, Tessa Monina, Beverley Smith and Roy Fox.